THE BARONE SYSTEM

55 YEARS SLIM
and
LIVING WELL

Anne Barone

THE ANNE BARONE COMPANY

The Barone System:
55 Years Slim and Living Well
Anne Barone

Published by The Anne Barone Company, Texas USA

ISBN: 978-1-937066-26-0
Printed in the United States of America

Book and Cover Design: Anne Barone
Cover Image: sebos/Shutterstock
Eiffel Tower Design: Joyce Wells/GriggsArt

This book is intended as philosophy and general reference only. It is not to be used as a substitute for medical advice or treatment. Every individual's problems with the aging process are unique and complex. You should consult your physician for guidance on any medical condition or health-issue and to make certain any product or treatment you use are right and safe for you.

The author and publisher disclaim any responsibility for any liability, loss or risk incurred directly or indirectly from the use or application of any of the contents of this publication or from any of the materials, machines, services or products mentioned in it.

The mention of specific companies, products, organizations or authorities in this book does not imply endorsement by the author or publisher, nor does mention of specific companies, products, organizations or authorities imply that they endorse this book, its author, or its publisher. Every effort has been made that internet addresses and other sources of information are accurate at the time of publication.

For more links and related information visit: *annebarone.com*

*To my grandmother Besse
and her sister, my great aunt Sudie
Though different, each provided a role model
for ageing well*

Contents

Chic & Slim Books by Anne Barone
Print and eBook

CHIC & SLIM:
How Those Chic French Women
Eat All That Rich Food And Still Stay Slim

CHIC & SLIM ENCORE:
More About How French Women Dress Chic Stay Slim
—and How You Can Too!

CHIC & SLIM TECHNIQUES:
10 Techniques To Make You Chic & Slim
à la française

CHIC & SLIM TOUJOURS:
Aging Beautifully Like Those Chic French Women

CHIC & SLIM TOUJOURS 2:
More Aging Beautifully Like Those Chic French Women

CHIC & SLIM CONNOISSEUR:
Using Quality To Be Chic Slim Safe & Rich

ARMOIRE BOUDOIR CUISINE & SAVVY:
Success Techniques For Wardrobe Relaxation
Food & Smart Thinking

About the Author Anne Barone

Once fat and frumpy, in her mid-20s Anne Barone began to learn chic French women's techniques for eating well and staying slim and for dressing chic on a small budget. She lost 55 pounds and acquired a chic French wardrobe.

Chicer and slimmer, Anne Barone returned to the USA to find a nation growing heavier and less chic. She decided to share her French secrets. In 1997, Anne Barone published her first French-inspired book *Chic & Slim: how those chic French women eat all that rich food and still stay slim*. Six more *Chic & Slim* books followed revealing even more French secrets for dressing chic and staying slim and healthy. *Chic & Slim Toujours* and *Toujours 2* focus on staying slim and healthy in women's middle and later years.

Now 80, Anne Barone has been slim and healthy for more than 55 years. She lives in Texas where she divides her time between writing and restoring an almost 100-year-old property.

You can learn more about Anne Barone and her books and lifestyle at the companion website *annebarone.com*.

aging / ageing

a clarification

Americans spell the word "aging." The British spell it "ageing."

In my two previous books, *Chic & Slim Toujours* and *Chic & Slim Toujours 2,* I used the American spelling for the word commonly used for that natural process of becoming older.

Since then I have recognized that the American spelling carries a possibility of confusion. Often in encountering "aging," my eyes read "again." The British spelling prevents that possible confusion.

So I have chosen to use "ageing" throughout this book.

55 Years Slim

LOSING WEIGHT IS EASY. It's staying slim that is difficult.

Each year millions of people shed unwanted fat and reach their goal weight. But it is maintaining that healthy slim weight year after year, decade after decade, that is difficult. For most of my lifetime this has been too difficult for the majority of people despite the number of medical aids and "diets." A good percentage of those who lost weight gained it back. Often they gained back more than they lost.

In my mid-20s, I lost 55 pounds. Now, having celebrated my 80th birthday, I have stayed slim for more than 55 years using the system I created by observing how chic French women kept their *ooh-la-la* figures.

Since I published the first *Chic & Slim* book in August 1997, I have written seven books about those French techniques. But France has changed and French women have changed since I was learning those chic and slim French lessons. French culture that I believe was the foundation for French women staying slim has undergone what the French political analyst Jérôme Fourquet has described as *les métamorphoses de la France*, the dramatic transformations in French culture that began in the 1980s and continue today.

Among France's many changes, under the influence—largely from watching American television programs—many French have adopted elements of American culture that produced the USA's surge in overweight and obesity with the resulting surge in overweight and obesity in France.

As a result, French women no longer provide the inspiration they did for me that half century ago. Sadly French women are neither as chic nor as slim as they used to be—with, of course, the marvelous exceptions. Mostly, I understand, Parisiennes. And a number of those are not French.

But during the course of writing this book in which I focus on how I lost weight and have stayed slim—particularly between ages 70 and 80—two major discoveries arrived to offer medical solutions for overweight and obesity.

The first to get attention was the discovery that the gut microbiome played a major role in determining whether an individual was slim or obese or somewhere in-between. These discoveries concerning the role played by bacteria in the digestive system helped explain why some people could "eat anything they wanted" and still stay slim. And why some people could suffer great hunger pains on a low calorie diet and hardly lose an ounce.

The results of this knowledge was that various medical experts recommended intermittent fasting. In this type of fasting, periods of eating alternate with periods of fasting during which those bacteria in the gut microbiome have time to do their work efficiently. In this book I describe my own experience with intermittent fasting. Not to lose weight. I did not need that. But as a possible solution to some stress-induced digestive problems I developed.

As a result of this new medical knowledge concerning the gut microbiome, several companies sprang up to offer medical testing and advice on determining the makeup of a person's microbiome and how by diet they might control their health—and their weight. Most notable of these was ZOE headquartered in the UK and co-founded by British medical doctor and science writer Tim Spector whose best selling books introduced millions to their gut microbiomes.

But the research into the gut microbiome and its connection to weight control was soon overshadowed by a truly momentous breakthrough: the discovery that drugs being used in the treatment of type 2 diabetes could be used off-label for substantial weight loss. *Ta-dah!* The weight loss "silver bullet" that had long been hoped for had arrived.

These drugs, GLP-1 receptor agonists, work by increasing insulin production, slowing digestion, reducing appetite and causing feelings of fullness. The first to come to world attention was Ozempic (semaglutide) made by the Danish company Novo Nordisk. The demand for Ozempic's use for weight loss became so heavy that those with type 2 diabetes for a time found themselves unable to procure the medicine. Novo Nordisk soon introduced Wegovy, a version of Ozempic to be used for weight loss.

But the real winner for the amount of weight that could be lost taking these drugs was tirzepatide made by the American Eli Lilly Company. Called Mounjaro as the type 2 diabetes version and Zepbound for weight loss.

These drugs were badly needed. Despite bariatric surgery and numerous other treatments, the world's obesity statistics had grown alarming higher—and higher. In 2024, the NCD Risk Factor

Collaboration published findings that estimate that more than one billion people in the world are now obese.

By the time the weight loss value of these originally type 2 diabetes drugs became known, medical studies had also determined that a key factor in this obesity epidemic was the food industry's development of ultra-processed foods designed to be addictive and unsatisfying. One did not reach 370, nor 500 pounds, confining one's eating to lean proteins, whole grains, fresh fruit and leafy green veggies.

Interestingly, as I learned how these weight loss miracle drugs worked, I realized that a major factor in my ability to stay slim long term was my avoidance of ultra-processed foods. As well as avoidance of those activities that enticed people to consume them.

By avoiding ultra-processed foods and by eating a diet rich in foods high in protein and fiber (eggs, nuts, whole grains, unsaturated fats) that had been identified as promoting the natural production of the GLP-1 hormone, my body was giving me the regulation of blood sugar levels, slowing of digestion and the feeling of fullness that Ozempic/Wegovy and Mounjaro/Zepbound gave people who took those medications—thankfully without negative side effects and without the very considerable expense.

Christopher Damman, Associate Professor of Gastroenterology, School of Medicine, University of Washington points out: "Specialized bacteria in your lower gut take the components of food you can't digest like fiber and polyphenols—the elements of plants that are removed in many processed foods—and transforms them into molecules that stimulate hormones to control your appetite and metabolism. These include GLP-1, a natural version of Wegovy and Ozempic. GLP-1 tells your brain that you've had enough to eat and your stomach and intestines to slow the movement of food along the digestive tract to allow for digestion."

In this book I outline in detail the eating plan that keeps me slim and healthy. Both what I eat and what I do not eat.

But the seriously obese are beyond natural remedies that might come from healthy eating. Weight loss drugs are badly needed because, without major intervention, over half the world's population is slated to be overweight or obese by 2030. That said, these drugs are still very expensive, must be self-administered by an injector pen, and of course, there are the much publicized unpleasant side effects that many users experience: diarrhea, vomiting, constipation. Rapid weight loss can cause the face to look older, the buttocks to sag, hair loss, and even rarely, pancreatitis demanding hospitalization. Oh, dear!

And what if you find you can no longer afford the medication or that you cannot tolerate the unpleasant side effects? If you quit cold turkey, then quite likely you will experience blood sugar spikes, increased appetite and, worst of all, you will regain the lost weight.

In any case, the good news is that most of the unpleasant side effects can be avoided or diminished by careful eating. Bad news: to get the ultimate benefit of these weight loss drugs you must also eliminate from your diet many of the foods that made you gain weight in the first place.

The biggest concern for women is that when these drugs produce rapid weight loss, it is not just fat that is lost. Very often the weight loss involves loss of muscle mass and bone density, special concerns for older women vulnerable to osteoporosis and falls. This muscle and bone density loss can sometimes be offset by resistance exercise and lots of lean protein. But since another side effect is fatigue, it may be hard to be faithful to those resistance exercises. Since the drugs diminish appetite, this can make it difficult to consume all the lean protein needed to combat the muscle and bone density loss.

Obviously the ultimate successful use of these drugs depends much on revamping one's lifestyle and eating habits. This is why I believe that the material in this book can help with the development of eating habits for a slim and healthy body whether you have the assistance of one of these miracle medications or not.

Of course, obesity carries so many risks that weight loss itself can greatly improve health. As more people use these drugs (one in eight people in the USA are said to have used Ozempic/Wegovy or Mounjaro/Zepbound) there are reports that these drugs also show evidence of reducing cognitive decline, dramatically improving knee osteoarthritis, and slowing ageing. Even the possibility to reduce addictions such as smoking, gambling, and overconsumption of alcohol.

Another benefit of these weight loss drugs is they have been found to reduce stress and anxiety. We know that stress itself can cause weight gain. In this book's chapter on stress, I describe how I have coped with stress to prevent it causing me to gain weight and how certain foods help the body cope with stress.

One thing, however, I have learned from my observations of people and their body weight is that many use their obesity to protect themselves from things they fear, or provide themselves with an excuse for not doing things they cannot do, or do not want to do.

I have read there is an idea in the UK to give those who are not working because of extreme obesity these new miracle weight loss medications. Then, their slimmer, healthier bodies will be able return to work and not only will the government save the money these people are receiving as welfare aid, but as employed workers they will be paying taxes to the government.

Somehow I don't think that people on government assistance now spending leisurely days on the couch in front of their televisions stuffing themselves on ultra-processed junk food are going to cheerfully inject themselves with a medication that will enable them to get up in the morning and go to work.

But there is no doubt that these medications—and others even more effective and less expensive and surely a pill version to be developed—will make a huge impact on our lives. Already airlines are being told that they may need less fuel for their planes because the weight of the passenger load will soon be considerably reduced.

For someone like me who has been focused on the dynamics of weight control for all of her adult life, it will be fascinating to observe what transpires. Not only in the matter of weight control, but also in the increasing evidence that these weight loss drugs may also slow ageing and prevent diseases ageing often brings.

Medical science already knows how to prolong lifespan. Hook the human body to enough machines and inject it with enough chemicals and it can be kept technically alive for a very long time. Healthspan, those years living a quality life without any major illness, is another matter. There have not been as spectacular medical discoveries for prolonging healthspan as these recent discoveries for weight control. But progress is being made. One medication that has shown promise is Metformin, interestingly another medication given to treat type 2 diabetes.

An article on the AARP (American Association of Retired Persons) website quoted Nir Barzilai, M.D., director of the Institute for Aging Research at the Albert Einstein College of Medicine in New York. "Metformin targets all the biological hallmarks of aging. It's also safe, has few side effects, it's generic, it's cheap." Additionally it comes in a pill. No painful injections required.

Even though Metformin and several other drugs are being seriously studied for their benefits to ageing, the research that has most interested me is that concerning how diet and lifestyle can slow ageing and increase one's healthspan. I discuss this relationship between diet, lifestyle and longevity in the Coping With Natural Ageing chapter.

But first we begin with what I do to stay slim—followed by what I never do. And a caution. As you read, you may find ideas you might use for staying slim and healthy. Keep in mind that everyone's body is unique. At any age, but especially as one becomes older, it is important that before you set about making changes in eating and exercise, you always follow the advice and direction of your medical advisor.

Things I Always Do

I Always Eat A Healthy Diet Appropriate For Me

Two truths I know about losing weight and staying slim longterm: What you eat matters. What you do NOT eat matters. Perhaps even more.

Furthermore, I know that medical research has confirmed that nutritional needs and how our bodies process food varies greatly among individuals. To stay slim and healthy we have to consider the best medical evidence, our own experience with food and health, and our doctor's advice as to what is best for our health condition. With these factors in mind, then we design a healthy diet that best suits our bodies' requirements and our lifestyles. Additionally, this diet must be feasible within our budget and can be purchased by local shopping or by ordering online. Of course, as we age, our bodies' nutritional needs and how our bodies process food change. And I can assure you that the way our bodies process food as we age will likely not change for the better.

Having unloaded all these caveats, what do I eat to stay slim and healthy?

In addition to learning French techniques for staying slim in my mid-20s, I believe equally important in enabling me to remain slim all these years was the influence of living several years on the Mediterranean. There I adopted a diet and a style of eating that I have continued through the decades. Today we know these foods and style of eating as the Mediterranean Diet, with its focus on whole grains, fresh produce, lean protein such as chicken and fish. And, of course extra virgin olive oil. In Mediterranean eating, foods are well-seasoned with herbs and spices that have antioxidant and anti-inflammatory benefits. This way of eating has repeatedly shown to give protection against health problems such as heart disease, metabolic syndrome, diabetes, dementia and depression—even some cancers, particularly colon, breast, and prostate cancers. In older adults this diet has been shown to give a decreased risk of frailty, an underlying cause of debilitating falls.

It was those years living on the Mediterranean with a view of the sea from every room of our villa, and the back garden gate opening onto the beach that I became a devotee of cooking with high quality olive oil. I even reached a point where I preferred croissants and pastries made with olive oil instead of butter. Here where the sun sparkled off the brilliant blue sea, ratatouille, *salade Niçoise*, bouillabaisse on which floated aïoli-topped toasted rounds of baguette, and the garbanzo flour bread *socca* became part of my diet that has continued to this day.

I don't make couscous as often now as I did. In any case, I can never make this meat and vegetable stew served over steamed semolina grains taste as good as that our maid would regularly prepare. And chickpeas. I became a devoted fan of chickpeas (garbanzo beans).

Who could not eat more healthily when orange trees in the front garden produced such juicy fruit and the big almond tree in the back garden gave us a profusion of pink blossoms in spring against an impossibly lovely background of aquamarine sea? And we would have enjoyed more of those almonds had the maid not eaten so many of the them green! We even had an olive tree. It did not produce many olives, but the little stores at the market had tubs brimming with both green and black varieties, seasoned and unseasoned.

Living on the Mediterranean, a whole new array of fish presented itself. I added Alan Davidson's classic *Mediterranean Seafood* with its wonderful drawings of the fish to my library of cookbooks. Guided by its pages I set forth to discover new fish and fish dishes. This lead to new seafood preparation adventures, including once being bitten by a barracuda.

Living on the Mediterranean I developed a preference for sheep and goat cheeses, said to be easier on the digestive system than those made from cow's milk. Though if cow's milk cheese presented any truly potent dangers, the French, cheese-eaters that they are, would surely all be dead.

While olive is my principal oil, for some cooking I also use canola oil or grape seed oil. Both have higher smoke points than olive oil, which in sautéing, if not carefully watched, can overheat. With canola or grape seed oil I am not so likely to set off the smoke alarm and scare the cat out of her wits. I love roasted walnut oil with balsamic vinegar and a bit of fig puree in a dressing for a spinach, pear and feta salad.

A staple of my diet for the last thirty years is *Caldo verde*, a traditional Portuguese soup whose recipe I found in a newspaper food section when I was writing the second *Chic & Slim* book. At the time I began making this kale soup, the white potatoes traditionally used were out of favor with nutritionists. I substituted millet for a while, then left the starch out entirely and instead accompanied my soup with a chunk of my homemade whole grain bread or with *socca*. I beef up the taste and nutrition of this soup with a dollop of plain Greek yogurt and a tablespoon or so of brewers yeast.

Lately my *Caldo verde* has undergone modification. When I learned that the greens used in the Portuguese soup (whose recipe dates back to the mid-15th century) was closer to our collard greens than kale, I switched to collards. The taste is different. But I am coming to enjoy it, especially since my reason for eating this soup is primarily for its high calcium content. According to the University of Rochester Medical Center data base, a cup of cooked kale has only 179 mg calcium while a cup of collards has 266 mg.

I want to eat a healthy diet because I want to maintain my healthspan, those years one remains healthy and disease-free. But how can I judge if I am eating the best healthy diet for me? Recently I learned about a way of eating that is considered by some as even better than the Mediterranean Diet in reducing a person's overall risk of early death. I must admit that in all my study of healthy eating I had not until this year heard of Harvard's Alternative Healthy Eating Index (AHEI). Not a catchy acronym, you must admit.

In any case, the Harvard medical people have come up with a questionnaire to help determine how well your regular diet conforms to this way of eating that has shown to reduce the risk of developing type 2 diabetes by 33 per cent and coronary heart disease (which can increase the risk of stroke and dementia) by 31 per cent.

In the past I have never done well on most diet evaluations. They always seem to require no grains, no dairy or caffeine (that eliminates my homemade bread, as well as yogurt and tea) or insists that one subsist on avocados and almonds or some other extremely restricted eating. So I approached Harvard's AHEI prepared for a low score.

Each factor offered a possible 10 points. A perfect score was 70. The factors were:

5 servings of vegetables a day — 10pts

4 servings of whole fruit a day — 10pts

5 servings of wholegrains a day — 10pts

Avoid all fruit juice and sugary drinks all week — 10pts

7 servings of nuts, soy and beans a week — 10pts

Avoid red and processed meat all week — 10pts

2 servings of fish a week — 10pts

I was flabbergasted at the results. I scored a perfect 70 points.

But then most days I eat more than five servings of vegetables. And always four of fruit. I had worried that the several slices of my homemade breads I eat most days would count against me. But no. And then the buckwheat, millet, and amaranth along with spelt, whole wheat, cornmeal easily make 5 servings of wholegrains. I never drink fruit juice or any beverage with sugar. The last time I ate beef was about six years ago. And thanks to my brother who keeps me supplied with fish (including wild caught halibut and salmon from a fishing trip to the Pacific waters off the coast of northern Alaska) I usually eat fish at least three meals per week.

I am sure that if my diet had not been so influenced by

Mediterranean foods and way of eating, I would not have done so well on Harvard's Alternative Healthy Eating Index evaluation.

The American Gut Project, as well as other recent studies, have confirmed that the more different plant types a person eats, the higher the microbial diversity of their gut. That microbial diversity can result in better physical health by playing an important role in the functioning of our immune system and combatting inflammation. It can also result in better mental health. That diversity can also help us stay slim.

Eating a diversity of foods is no problem for me. I love a wide variety of foods and cuisines from many different cultures. I have often said that I had never found a cuisine that I did not like. To this, a woman familiar with Tibet said obviously I had never tasted anything cooked in fermented yak butter.

There are a couple of popular ways to check that you are eating enough fruits and vegetables as well as a diversity of foods. The 10 Fruits and Vegetables Per Day lets you count almost all fruits, but for vegetables you cannot count any kind of potatoes, nor corn (it's a grain) nor, of course, any nuts or seeds. I try not to be too much of a purist about this count. But I will admit on occasions when I calculate that my supper salad will only bring the count to nine, going out and poking around between the roses and the daylilies and bringing in enough wild violet leaves to make the tally 10.

The 30 Plants Per Week count is advocated by Tim Spector, British geneticist, microbiome expert and co-founder of the personalized nutrition company ZOE designed to help members make smarter food choices for overall health.

For the 30 Plants Per Week you count all the fruits and vegetables plus nuts, seeds, grains, beans, all the pulses (dried version of beans and peas.) You can even count tea and coffee. Dr. Spector even allows counting different varieties of wine. Obviously, even if you eat almonds as well as almond butter, you can only count the almonds once. But if you eat red grapes and green grapes, each count separately as do various varieties of beans and peas. I usually exceed the 30 total by two or three. Often more.

If you don't do these counts already, try them. I find them fun and they keep me aware of what I am eating on a regular basis. These counts are certainly a way to encourage eating a diversity of foods to benefit your mental and physical health. This eating diversity can also help you stay slim.

I Always Eat Breakfast

I don't think there has been a morning of my life when I skipped breakfast, except when necessitated by some medical procedure that required fasting after midnight. During that period in my mid-20s when I was losing those 55 pounds, my usual breakfast was the classic French breakfast: a *tartine*, that is, a chunk of baguette spread with butter and jam or marmalade and a cup of strong French roast coffee to which I added a little Nestlé *lait écrémé en poudre*, the powdered skim milk that I found such a great improvement over the instant non-fat dry milk that I drank in my fatty days growing can you up in the USA. But by the time I began writing the *Chic & Slim* books in my late 40s, my breakfasts had undergone modification.

When I wrote *Chic & Slim Encore*, the second *Chic & Slim* book, I was baking and eating an all whole wheat version of Irish Soda Bread with my morning coffee. (Tea then was still only drunk with my afternoon tea.) I ate the bread with butter and jam or honey. Especially a wild honey from the mountains of Jamaica of which I became very fond. A couple of years later that bread had metamorphosed into something more like Logan Bread, a high protein, high fiber bread. It is claimed that a small square of Logan Bread will sustain you for a full day of mountain climbing up Mount Logan.

Then in my mid-60s I found myself requiring more substance and more protein to start my day. My breakfast menu began to include a soft-boiled egg. And my breakfast bread had undergone another metamorphosis. Now I was baking my Barone Breakfast Bread. This was another high protein, high fiber bread I baked in the oven in my trusty cast iron skillet. The composition always included three parts rolled oats to which I would add 1 part of 3 different flours. These varied between buckwheat, rye, sorghum, teff, oat, garbanzo, amaranth, brown rice flour, and flaxseed meal depending on what I had on hand. And my whim. The dough included baking powder, milk, eggs and oil, usually canola. Also I began adding shredded carrots as a way to include a vegetable in my breakfast.

But when, a couple of years ago, my faithful 75-year-old gas kitchen range oven ceased working properly, I had to give up the Barone Breakfast Bread and bake all my bread in my bread machine. Most often this is a bread made from organic sprouted spelt flour, sometimes with, sometimes without organic flaxseed meal. So for the past year or so it has been a soft boiled egg and one slice spelt-flax toast. To top the toast, I alternate between organic butter and organic flax seed oil — with my homemade stevia-sweetened jam.

The point of this enumeration of my evolving breakfasts over my decades of slim is that you can eat a variety of breakfasts and still stay slim. That said, I have known far more chic, slim women who either skipped breakfast or simply had a cup or tea or coffee perhaps with some fruit. But breakfast for me MUST include some sort of bread and hot caffeine.

Those of you familiar with my *Chic & Slim* books and articles know that Anne Barone thinks dry breakfast cereal is NOT CHIC. My prejudice is founded in my fatty days when I breakfasted on bowls of Special K believing the hype that these dry tasteless flakes drowned in non-fat milk and sweetened with artificial sweetener (cyclamate in those days before the FDA banned it) was my way to slimness. It wasn't. I found a better way, but my prejudice against dry cereal remains.

This prejudice, however, does not extend to cooked cereal such as oatmeal. In fact, hot oatmeal breakfasts sustained me through the Texas Freeze of 2021 when our electrical grid failed. (During much of that electrical outage my bathroom was 10 degrees F. colder than the inside of my refrigerator. Chilly.)

Today nutritional experts suggest that the ideal breakfast is a bowl of oatmeal with a few blueberries—and perhaps some walnuts. For me, hot oatmeal is okay in extremely cold weather. But on most mornings? No.

In cold weather what I prepare for an oatmeal breakfast involves cooking old-fashioned rolled oats with cinnamon, flaxseed meal, raisins, and chopped pecans, then served with flaxseed oil plus a dash of stevia. If I am honest, I admit I am effectively eating an oatmeal cookie with a spoon. That is bad enough. But even though this concoction tastes wonderful, I still feel like a peasant hunched over a bowl slurping gruel. Not chic. And for me, chic has always been a strong motivation for slim.

I Always Bake and Eat Healthy Homemade Bread

Let me say first of all, if there is something that you really love that has the potential to cause you to gain weight, then make sure that you are eating the healthiest, tastiest version possible. That is why I bake (almost) all my own bread.

I am not sure who invented the Bread Machine, but on my list of those to whom I feel gratitude and admiration, they come in the Top Ten along with the inventors of the air conditioner and the flush toilet. Bread machines make it so much easier to have delicious, healthy bread. Because the reality is that most American supermarket bread is made with too much salt, too much sugar, too many chemicals, and mostly made from low-quality flours. American supermarket bread little resembles what the rest of the world eats as bread.

Artisan bread equivalent to the world's best is available in the USA. But, unfortunately in most of the places I have lived this quality of bread was either unavailable or beyond my budget. But with a bread machine and the high-quality flours I order, I can bake and eat a variety of breads that both delight my palate and provide excellent nutrition.

My bread recipes have evolved through the years and I am constantly trying new ones. Since age 75, the bread I make most often is from an organic sprouted whole grain spelt with some organic flaxseed meal. Very healthy. And since I love coarse, dark breads, I find it delicious.

Spelt is an ancient relative of our modern wheat flour. I love spelt bread's nutty taste and, like many people, I find spelt breads and other baked goods easier to digest. The sprouted version of spelt flour has added benefits in that sprouting the spelt grains before grinding into flour reduces the percentage of starch and increases that of the protein. I especially like that spelt bread does not require as much kneading as wheat and rye and other breads. Once you mix the dough and let it rise once in the baking pan, it is ready to bake.

I Always Exercise

Even in my fatty days, I exercised. Since I lost those 55 pounds, exercise has been an important part of the lifestyle that has kept me slim and healthy. For the first 30 years after I became slim, my exercise was, for the most part, walking and swimming. Though in the 1980s, I added exercise videos beginning with Jane Fonda's original workout. For the past 20 plus years my exercise has been walking, exercise DVDs—and for about 15 of these years, a treadmill when outdoor exercise would not be pleasant. Where I live, a good part of the year the weather is not pleasant.

Those of you who follow my website *annebarone.com* know that I have now replaced my treadmill with an exercise bicycle, an appliance which arrived in a refrigerator-sized box, and the assembly of whose multitude of parts gave me great challenge. But I did finally get the thing put together and in use.

The older I become, the more important physical exercise is for staying slim and healthy. And for keeping my brain working well. The list of exercise benefits for ageing people is lengthy: preventing bone loss, relieving arthritis pain, preventing chronic disease, boosting immunity and improving our mental state. Sadly, too many older Americans spend a great part of their time sitting in front of a television with a remote control in hand.

For my 70th birthday, a fan of my *Chic & Slim* books and website gave me Miranda Esmonde-White's book *Aging Backwards: 10*

Years Younger, 10 Years Lighter, 30 Minutes a Day plus the DVD set for the author's *Classical Stretch: Strength & Flexibility.* Bless you, Susan. The book and the DVDs have turned out to be the next best thing to having the Fountain of Youth installed in my garden. Miranda Esmonde-White's exercise programs have been as useful to my successful ageing as the techniques I learned from French women were useful to losing 55 pounds and staying slim.

The other exercise DVD that I alternated with the Miranda Esmonde-White programs was Jennifer Kries' *The New Method Pilates Precision Toning and Sculpting.* This DVD was recommended to me by mother and daughter fans of the *Chic & Slim* books. I began using the program not long after its original release in 1996. Unfortunately even used copies are almost impossible to find these days. But the program really does sculpt and tone. From time to time, however, for some reason of another, I get out of the routine of regularly doing this Pilates workout. My body quickly shows it.

Because I spend so much time sedentary working at my computer, I must balance these seated work sessions with walking. My exercise bicycle gets the heartbeat up (and it is equipped with a desk so I can read or write while pedaling), but walking brings a multitude of benefits I need for healthy ageing. Walking improves circulation and blood pressure, keeps muscles, bones and joints strong and the brain functioning well to help fend off dementia and Alzheimer's.

The walking recommendation for women 62-101 years is 30 minutes per day, five days a week, or 7500 steps per day. Some days I think I get half of those 7500 steps just walking to the door to let the cat in and out of the house.

One thing that has been observed in all the regions that have the highest concentration of people who have lived beyond 100 years, is that these long-lived healthy individuals have physical activity as part of their daily routine: whether for going to their work or for daily errands, gardening, or other manual labor activities.

While a fair portion of my half-acre property is flowers, ground cover, trees and shrubs, there is still a LOT of grass to mow. Up until about four years ago, I used an electric push mower. Since then I use a rechargeable battery-powered Ryobi self-propelled lawn mower. It has a speed regulator which I can set for a nice brisk walk. With the mild climate here at *Provence-sur-la-Prairie*, the growing season for grass is long. During respites from lawn maintenance, usually in winter or in one of our periodic droughts, I have a walking track laid out for which the privacy fence gives nice protection from the harsh wind on cold days. And there is enough light from neighbors' security lights that I can walk safely in cooler hours after dark in very hot weather.

Exercise is necessary for staying healthy and slim. But you have to do it. Everyday.

I Always Avoid Plastics As Much As Possible

When the information about the dangers of plastics and microplastics recently began to appear in the media, I took satisfaction in my belief I was far ahead of most people. After all, I had been avoiding plastics, especially plastics that came in contact with food, since the early 1970s. Though, as I remember, the avoidance of plastic then was more part of the "back to the natural and traditional" effort, than based on the scientific evidence of dangers from plastic we now have.

In any case, it turns out that I am not as far ahead at avoiding plastics as I thought. Some product choices I was making to avoid consuming foods that come packaged in plastics turned out to expose the foods to plastic after all.

What a shock to learn that those "waxed paper" milk cartons were not waxed. Wax had been used in the first paper milk cartons but today that wax has been replaced with a thin coat of polyethylene. That's plastic. But the greatest shock was learning that teabags without staples, strings and tags, actually contain plastics (for sealing the bag together). Increasingly I had been using more bagged teas for their convenience. Back to loose leaf teas and only stringed teabags.

The scientific evidence of the dangers of plastics and microplastics is irrefutable. Many plastics in extensive use today pose serious health hazards, particularly from two sorts of chemicals: phthalates and bisphenols.

Phthalates are endocrine-disrupting chemicals that can damage the liver, kidneys, lungs, and reproductive system. Developing fetuses and the young are particularly vulnerable. Phthalates are often used in personal care products such as soaps, shampoos and hair sprays. You may have them in your house in vinyl flooring, plastic packages or, as I do, water pipes.

At some expense I had all the old leaking copper water pipes replaced with PVC. But I was encouraged to learn that boiling removes phthalates from water. Much of water I drink is boiled for making tea. Each time I make tea, I boil extra water that I can cool and bottle in glass bottles for drinking water.

As for bisphenols, like phthalates, they are hormone disrupters and are present in a multitude of products, though we get our greatest exposure to them in packaged food and beverages. A link has been found between bisphenol exposure and increased risk of cardiovascular diseases, neurological disorders, reproductive abnormalities, diabetes—and obesity. Because bisphenols are used so extensively and their discharge is so long-term, bisphenols pose a serious problem for our health.

Fortunately, the concerns about plastics and microplastics have generated a wealth of articles that alert us to what products give us serious exposures to the more dangerous of these and guide us in our avoidance. Though I am not sufficiently concerned to follow the advice to swap out my conventional plastic toothbrush for one with a wooden handle and a head made of pig bristles.

I Always Have Afternoon Tea

As I explained in the introduction to this book, while the techniques I used to lose fat and keep the pounds from coming back were in large part based on French techniques, there were things that were a major help to me that were not (much) in the French repertoire. Afternoon tea is one example.

Afternoon tea is a British custom, though how many in the UK regularly follow this custom today is, I understand, much less than in the past. I was introduced to the custom when I was a Peace Corps Volunteer in West Africa by the British Ambassador's wife there.

Shortly after, one of women officers at the American Embassy gave me a package of green tea that Chinese friends in Hong Kong had given her as a going-away gift when she finished her tour of duty at the American Embassy there. She was not a tea drinker, but she had learned enough about tea while living in Hong Kong that she knew this was an expensive and special tea. She gave it to me saying she believed I would enjoy it. And I certainly did.

I loved the taste and made a special ritual of drinking it late afternoons on weekends when I was not working. No doubt the quality of this Chinese green tea made me realize that the Lipton's tea I had drunk as iced tea growing up was a far inferior version of tea than this lovely Chinese green I was enjoying.

After the Chinese green tea was finished, there was an interlude in my afternoon tea drinking until a year or so later when I went to live in India. The Indians were even more devoted tea drinkers than the British. Besides a considerable part of the world's tea was grown on the hills of India's Assam and Darjeeling regions. My afternoon tea habit was established shortly after I arrived in New Delhi in the early 1970s. It has continued uninterrupted since.

Afternoon tea is not a snack. Afternoon tea is my stress-reliever and energy restorer. As my mood takes me, the tea drunk could be black, green, oolong or herbal teas. Lately I have had an opportunity to drink white tea. Elegant and lovely. What tea I drink will also depend on what nibble I plan to accompany the tea.

Green tea is generally considered to be the healthiest of the *Camellia sinensis* teas. Green tea is usually touted as superior in health benefits to black or oolong teas. But more recent studies conclude that black teas have many health benefits as well.

A statement on cancer.gov, an official US government website, says: "A prospective study of half a million tea drinkers in the United Kingdom found health benefits from black tea. People who consumed two or more cups per day had a 9% to 13% lower risk of death from any cause than people who did not drink tea. Higher tea consumption was also associated with a lower risk of death from cardiovascular disease, ischemic heart disease, and stroke."

Surely they meant "early death." Drinking tea will not make you live forever. But my afternoon teas do make my life more pleasant and less stressful.

Oolong, lightly fermented, comes somewhere between green and black teas in health benefits. Herbal tea benefits vary with the herb from which the tea in made. Peppermint for digestion. Chamomile for digestion and sleep. Ginger for digestion. Fennel for strengthening eyesight, regulating hormones, improving digestion, and aiding memory—or so it has been long believed.

But my afternoon tea ritual is more than just a pot of hot tea and some tasty bit of food. My tea reading is an equally important element. Afternoon tea is when I read for pleasure. For a half hour or so I shut out whatever is worrying, annoying, or distressing me. (There always seems to be something!) Stress can cause weight gain. Afternoon tea is my destresser par excellence. Afternoon tea helps me stay slim.

I Always Eat Meals At Regular Times

Skipping a meal is something I can never remember doing. I enjoy eating and NOTHING ever seems to dent my appetite. In my process of working out my own version of chic French women's techniques for staying slim, I discovered that having my breakfast, lunch, afternoon tea and supper at approximately the same time each day was best for staying slim. And, of course, like chic French women, I did not snack between meals. These meals eaten at regular times a day have varied throughout the years as demanded by my lifestyle at the time and whether I had to accommodate the schedules of others.

Then a couple of years ago, I became aware of a new element to consider in the timing of my meals. Initially I wrote off intermittent fasting as the latest "health fad *du jour.*" At that time it was mostly touted as a means for losing weight. Well I didn't need intermittent fasting for that! After all, I had shed 55 pounds and stayed slim for a half century just eating real food in moderate portions and regularly getting some exercise, totally avoiding any of diets and exercise regimes that had soared to popularity then vanished from the scene. Why would I want to limit my eating window to only 8 hours out of 24? Or, as some were advocating, eating only five days out of seven?

But not long afterwards I became aware of the research being done on the gut microbiome, that complex ecosystem of microbes that live in the intestine. Intermittent fasting research showed evidence of its having a beneficial effect on those estimated 38 million microbes in that ecosystem.

Having periods of putting nothing more into our digestive systems than water or black tea or coffee would give our bodies time to perform the repair and maintenance needed to keep our gut microbiomes in proper working order to strengthen our immune systems, and in doing so, lessen our risk of diseases such as diabetes, arthritis, allergies and cancer. A properly working gut microbiome might also give us more years of healthy disease-free living. A longer healthspan.

At that time my regular eating was early rising at 5 or 5:30 AM, sipping hot tea for an hour or so as I read the news online. Then breakfast and nothing until a noontime lunch except a cup of black tea mid-morning. Afternoon tea was usually at 4 PM, sometimes 5 PM. Supper would begin about 6:30, sometimes as late 7:00 PM. Though this meal is never a large, I prefer a leisurely supper rarely consumed in less than an hour.

In my first effort at intermittent fasting, no matter if I was up by 4:30 or 5:00 AM, I began to try to delay breakfast until 6:00 AM and to finish my evening meal by 7:00 PM. That was a 13 hour eating window and an 11 hour fast. If those little microbiome critters had a problem with that, they would just had to work faster.

About the time I began trying to limit my eating window to 13 hours, I read an interview article with former French first lady Carla Bruni Sarkozy. She of the reed thin body explained that each morning she sipped a cup of hot water for the first hour after waking. Ms. Bruni-Sarkozy commented that drinking the water made her "feel so light."

I tried the water only first hour after waking in place of my usual tea. I did not feel "light." I felt groggy without caffeine. But I have persisted with the hot water only for an hour after waking. My stomach seems happier when I don't hit it empty with all those tea tannins.

In early March 2024 I became aware of the research done by University of Southern California biogerontologist Valter Longo on the connection between diet and longevity. Dr. Longo stated in a media interview: "We know [from research] that 16 hours or longer of daily fasting, particularly if they involve skipping breakfast, are associated with a shorter, not longer, lifespan and increased cardiovascular disease and other conditions."

Dr. Longo believes people should fast for 12 hours per day. That leaves a 12 hour eating window. Whew! Because that is just about all I can manage. As for his Fasting Mimicking Diet FMD, this diet, recommended to be followed several times a year, in which you limit your food intake to about 800 calories per day, and on which you eat only plant-based foods that are low sugar, low protein and contain a prescribed composite of nutrients, is not recommended for those over 65. Thank goodness. Those five-day FMDs did not sound like fun, but I do like the idea of living healthy as I age. And I do notice with the 12:12 eating, that my digestion is better and I generally feel more alert and energetic. And annoyed.

I wake up hungry whether I wake up at 4 or 7 AM. Since I usually am in bed by 10 PM and it is recommended to finish your evening meal three to four hours before bedtime, the 12:12 schedule I have worked out is no food before 7 AM and to finish the evening meal by 7 PM.

But like many older people, I am often wide awake by 4 or 5 AM. Delaying breakfast until 7 AM means I am spending time trying to distract myself from my hunger. Not fun.

The delayed breakfast is bad enough, but keeping an eye on the clock to make sure I have swallowed my last bite by 7 PM seems totally uncivilized.

I plan to continue the 12:12 for a while and, of course, continue my Mediterranean Diet style eating. Yet I am aware that research into the gut microbiome and intermittent fasting's benefits for health and longevity is still very new. Further, much of the research thus far has been done on yeast, rats and mice. Though the recent ZOE Big Intermittent Fasting Study did involve over 100,000 real live humans. Still, in the long term, intermittent fasting might turn out to be just another "health fad *du jour.*" Remember when they promised us our health salvation lay in oat bran?

I Always Fulfill My Nutritional Needs

Without proper nutrition our bodies have difficulty staying healthy. And as recent research shows, difficulty maintaining a healthy weight. I have to eat right to stay healthy and slim.

I have long tried to meet my nutritional needs through what I eat and drink. But as study after study has shown, especially beyond 70 years, it is difficult to meet all the ageing body's nutritional needs through food. Basically the reason for this is that ageing makes it more difficult to absorb nutrients from foods at the same time that the body's nutritional needs increase. Supplements may be useful, even necessary, for optimum health. And for staying slim.

Today an astonishing number of nutritional supplements are available. If you have a physician or nutritional advisor, one or the other, or both, will be your best source for guidance on whether you need supplements. And, if you do, which of the many you need. If you set out to supplement on your own, determining your personal needs, determining what will help but not harm you is of primary importance. I approached nutritional supplementation, as I do most things: Very Cautiously. And gradually. And after studying a great deal of information from reputable sources.

After my hysterectomy in my mid-40s, my primary care physician who was also the obstetrician-gynecologist who had done my surgery, prescribed Citracal Plus, a calcium supplement which, at that time, contained, in addition to calcium citrate, some magnesium, copper, manganese and boron. About 10 years ago I discovered reading my label on my new bottle of Citracal Plus that the magnesium was no longer included. This puzzled me because for your body to use calcium you also need magnesium.

After some research I discovered that the removal of the magnesium was most likely because the latest medical studies showed that calcium and magnesium should not be taken at the same time.

In any case, when I had been writing the *Chic & Slim* books in the early 1990s, I had read the comments of one chic French woman about how she had always taken magnesium for skin and nerves. Even with the hormone replacement therapy I was taking, I still had acne-prone skin. I began taking about 400 mg of magnesium citrate daily. Soon afterward, I added 500 mg of L-lysine. (Often referred to as just lysine.) Like my mother, I was prone to those breakouts on lips called "fever blisters" or sometimes, "cold sores." Whatever. They were painful and looked hideous. Lysine was touted as a preventative. Works for me. I have found through the years that as long as I maintain my 500 mg lysine per day regime, I suffer no breakouts on my lips. If I stop for a month or two, back they come.

About a decade ago, reports appeared in the media tells us that we should meet all our calcium needs from food instead of supplements. For decades doctors had been prescribing calcium supplements for postmenopausal women for osteoporosis prevention—as my doctor had done. When the controversy settled down, doctors acknowledged that it was difficult for most women to meet all their calcium needs from food, and some of this need could be met by a supplement.

Calcium citrate is recommended as the most easily tolerated by the body. Though calcium carbonate is most often found in "calcium supplements." That said, calcium needs vitamin D to be absorbed. Users of calcium supplements also need to be aware that the body cannot absorb more than about 500 mg at a time and daily intake of calcium also needs magnesium. The recommendation is the for 1,200 mg of calcium, the body needs 600 IUs of vitamin D, 320 mg of magnesium plus about 90 micrograms (mcg) of vitamin K. Oversupplementing with calcium has its dangers.

In any case, calcium, magnesium and lysine made up my supplement regime until about age 65 when I found that I did not have the energy I had previously enjoyed. I began taking a multivitamin formulated for those over 50. That did the trick as far as energy was concerned. Then at about 70, I began to think ahead. Like the French actress Jeanne Moreau, I wanted to "die in perfect health."

When I was living on the Texas Gulf Coast writing the first two *Chic & Slim* books, I had a friend there who had begun taking CoQ10 at age 70 to maintain her energy when she was caring for her terminally-ill daughter. Now I was 70, she was 100, living alone, and still driving herself to shopping. She credited CoQ10 for her healthy longevity.

Our cells use CoQ10 for growth and maintenance. But as we age, natural levels of this antioxidant decrease. To maintain optimum levels requires supplementation. After research convinced me the supplement was safe for me, I began with 100 mg of CoQ10 daily with hopes that my later years would be as active and mentally alert as that of my Corpus Christi friend. As I approached 80, I switched to 100 mg of ubiquinol, the active, more bioavailable form of CoQ10. Will I make it to a healthy 100? We shall see.

As I wrote earlier, my approach to nutritional supplementation is cautious. Before I buy and try any nutritional supplement, I do much research in reliable sources. Marketing for nutritional supplements today is omnipresent and persuasive—much of it unsubstantiated by valid testing.

I restrict my supplement information sources (with an occasional exception) to five: reports available on the website of the US National Institutes of Health, that of the Mayo Clinic, *healthline.com*, WebMD and *ConsumerLab.com*. This later is a much-recommended provider of independent test results and information to help consumers and healthcare professionals evaluate health and nutrition products.

Beyond my caution about sources of supplement information, I stick to products from well-known and respected supplement companies. One helpful feature of my *ConsumerLab.com* subscription is alerts to recalls and warnings from the FDA when certain products have been found to cause illnesses, sometimes death. But I have found that often a *ConsumerLab.com* "Top Pick" is not right for me. Some contain additional ingredients I have identified as problematic for me—usually that they cause gas and or bloating. I check ingredient lists on labels, but usually buy a product that *ConsumerLab.com* has tested. This testing gives me information about possible heavy metals, or if the supplement really contains what is listed on the label. Many times they don't.

With some supplements, trying different brands of that supplement may be necessary. French women take grape seed extract for varicose veins. When I, like my mother and grandmother, began having problems with unsightly veins on my legs, I tried more than a dozen different brands of grape seed extract before I identified the brand and the dosage that worked for me.

Two vitamins identified as likely requiring a supplement for many older people are vitamin B-12 and vitamin D-3. Vitamin B-12 is important for bone health and preventing cardiovascular disease, as well for slowing cognitive decline. Unfortunately, as bodies age, they lose the ability to absorb B-12 from foods well. Fortunately, B-12 is available in liquid form and often in heavy concentration. One or two drops a day costing only a few pennies may be all that is necessary to meet your need.

As I mentioned previously in this section, vitamin D-3 is especially important for older women. Sunscreens guard our skin against skin cancer, but at the same time, they hamper our ability to get our vitamin D via time spent in sunshine. In this case, supplementing is necessary. As with calcium, oversupplementing can be dangerous.

I do not take any prescription medications. But if, in the future, a health condition would require one, I would need to check to see if any supplement I might be taking would be contraindicated when taking the med. For example several cholesterol-lowering statin drugs can be affected by supplements. St. John's wort, when taken with atorvastatin (Lipitor), may actually result in increased cholesterol levels.

When taking supplements, you also must be aware that some supplements must not be taken at the same time as others. One may interfere with the absorption of another.

None of the minerals: calcium, magnesium, iron, zinc should be taken within two hours of another. Zinc should not be taken with a high fiber meal. Vitamin A, vitamin D, lycopene, zeaxanthin, and lutein must be taken with a meal high in fats, but not with calcium or magnesium. Vitamin K and vitamin E should not be taken at the same time.

You must work out your schedule of when each of your supplements is taken. Otherwise, you may be wasting your money and not deriving benefit from them.

Now you know those things that I always do. Had I not done them I do not believe I could have stayed slim these past more than 55 years. But as I have continually stressed in all my books and other writing our bodies are so individual and unique that there is no one system that brings success for every person. My hope is that these things that have contributed to my success in staying slim more than a half century will give you ideas for perfecting your own system that works for YOU.

Yet equally important as these things I always do to stay slim are those things that I never do. The following chapter tells you what I avoid.

Things I Never Do

I Never Eat Foods Containing Sugar

These days I eat no refined sugar. Okay, almost no refined sugar. In real life today it is impossible to avoid all sugar in its various manifestations. But arriving at this point of avoiding almost all sugar in my diet has been a long journey of gradually reducing the amount. And I am happy to report the process has been surprisingly easy. I credit this elimination of sugar from my diet with playing a major role in keeping me healthy and slim. Medical science now confirms that by reducing or eliminating sugar from our diet, we substantially lower our risk of high blood pressure, obesity and diabetes. In doing so we lower three of the main factors in developing heart disease, the leading cause of death in the USA and worldwide.

When I read the reports of studies on this relationship between sugar and disease, I remember the amount of sugar I consumed as a child and teenager and I am surprised that I am not riddled with health problems. Or, by this time, dead.

What saved me, I believe, is that in my mid-20s, when I began losing weight by changing my eating habits to ones more like those of chic French women, a key component of this transition was reducing the amount of sugar I ate. Reducing, not eliminating. After all, there were all those glorious French pastries to enjoy. In moderation, of course.

In those days, some half-century ago, the problems with sugar were chiefly identified as causing excess weight and dental problems. Now this half century later, medical evidence assures us that overconsumption of sugar not only can make us overweight and rot our teeth, but it puts us more at risk of developing heart disease, type 2 diabetes, chronic inflammation—even some cancers. Overconsumption can also contribute to arthritis and joint pain. Furthermore, the dangers of sugar become more pronounced after age 35. Fortunately by that age I had greatly reduced the amount of sugar in my daily food intake. The last time I drank a sugared, carbonated soft drink I was in my early 30s. That was a long time ago.

At this point a clarification is necessary to point out the difference between the various forms of sugar (used in processed and junk foods, and certainly in homebaked cakes, cookies, pies and other dishes), and in natural sugars found in foods, particularly in fruit. The human body does needs natural sugar to function well. In fruits this natural sugar comes in combination with other important nutrients. Think of the antioxidants in fruit. What the body does not need are all those forms of sugar that the food industry increasingly adds to ultra-processed and junk foods.

Additionally, the food industry is very clever about using technical names for sugar in the hope the watchful consumer will be fooled. But barley malt, dextrose, turbinado, lactose, maltose, malt syrup, Florida crystals, agave nectar, agave syrup, rice syrup, evaporated cane juice, and ethyl maltol are among the estimated more than 50 forms of sugar currently in use. In shopping, you must become a tireless and persistent label reader if you want to reduce or eliminate sugar.

In my years growing up fatty, it was customary in our family, all meals, except for breakfast, ended with a dessert. Though even if we ate no "dessert" with breakfast, we ate quantities of syrup on pancakes, honey on biscuits, and homemade jams and jellies on toast. As for the desserts, my family frowned on "factory" cookies, cakes and pies. So there was always a big supply of homemade. From the French I learned to end my meals, not with a high calorie sugared dessert, but with a piece of fresh fruit. Or a bit of cheese and fruit. Such an enormous reduction in my daily consumption of sugar.

Despite all the sugar that the food industry adds to food products, since I do not eat ultra-processed or junk food, nor drink sugared carbonated soft drinks, I have little difficulty avoiding the added sugars that are causing such havoc with Americans' health —as well as the health of people all over the world.

Done gradually, the process of eliminating sugar from the diet is easy and self-perpetuating. I achieved transitioning from sugar-sweetened food to stevia-sweetened by a gradual process over a period of months in which I replaced an increasing amount of regular sugar in my food with stevia. Now I have arrived at a point that, if I eat cakes or pies or other deserts made with refined sugar, I feel wretched. When you eat very little refined sugar as I do, even just one of your sister's homemade cookies might be enough to cause a Sugar Hangover. Not as bad as a hangover from too much alcohol, but sufficiently unpleasant to cause you, as you lie there in your bed sleepless and miserable in your mid-section, repeat over and over: I will never eat a Double Fudge Coconut Walnut Cookie again.

Don't I miss cakes, pies, cookies, all those sweet treats I overate in the fatty period of my life? No, because I bake cakes, pies, muffins, cookies. All without sugar. The sweetness comes from stevia that I add when serving, often accompanied by fruit. Over the years I have converted my favorite recipes and created new ones. My chocolate amaranth brownies are not only delicious, but totally without sugar. They are a high protein, high fiber, healthy as well as elegant dessert especially when I top them with dark cherries.

The chief problem with stevia for many people is that you cannot add it before baking. And if you see a package of stevia labeled "great for baking" it is not real 100% stevia. The only stevia that works to keep me slim is 100% pure organic stevia extract powder. And none of the brands sold locally meet this criteria. I must order.

Of the stevia brands sold locally some list maltodextrin (that's sugar and worse it can make you gassy) as the principal ingredient. Others list erythritol first. One brand sold as stevia is actually erythritol with only 4% stevia. True, erythritol is a sugar substitute that is considered generally safe. But recent research has linked long-term use to an increased risk of heart attack and stroke. I am glad I have used caution in the use of this sugar alcohol synthesized from corn using enzymes and fermentation.

But even all the 100% organic stevia extract powders are not the same. Several years ago the brand I had used for years changed sources of stevia leaf and the taste went from sweet to pucker-your-mouth bitter. I had to find another brand. The only version of a stevia plus other sweetener that is acceptable to me is one that combines inulin with stevia extract powder. Inulin is a prebiotic that helps beneficial gut bacteria to grow. It occurs naturally in a number of foods, but most used as a supplement has been extracted from chicory. On its own inulin has a subtle sweetness in tea and coffee.

Obesity, diabetes, heart problems. These are serious possibilities from the overconsumption of refined sugar. But there is another problem that sugar can cause: Eating too much sugar can make us LOOK OLD. Horrors!

When I began to read about this problem, I wondered if perhaps my avoidance of sugar is one reason that I now at 80 have few wrinkles in comparison with many women my age. Medical research has discovered glycation, a process by which sugar in your bloodstream attaches to proteins to form harmful new molecules. The researchers named these new molecules Advanced Glycation End Products, AGEs for short. A more youthful appearance is such a bonus for avoiding sugar.

I Never Eat Ultra-Processed And Junk Foods

For a while we called them Frankenfoods. Unnatural edible substances created by the food industry for the purpose of making a profit. Then in 2010, a team of Brazilian scientists searching for the causes of the obesity epidemic came up with a more scientific name: ultra-processed foods (often abbreviated now as UPFs). Ultra-processed to distinguish them from plain old processed foods where real food (and little else) had been put in a can, or ground into flour and put in a bag, or meat butchered. In the original *Chic & Slim* book subtitled *How Those Chic French Women Eat All That Rich Food And Still Stay Slim*, I gave you an example an ultra-processed food: American supermarket bread that contained 16 ingredients, a good percentage of which were chemicals. I compared it with the French baguette which, by law, must contain only flour, water, salt and yeast. Another clue to identifying UPFs is that they usually list more than five ingredients on the label including emulsifiers, modified starches, thickeners, bulking agents, artificial sweeteners, food coloring, and flavoring. The flavoring always seems to be listed as "natural flavoring."

I once called the 800 number listed on a product label and asked what the "natural flavoring" listed on the label was. The customer service rep connected me to someone in the company's lab who admitted that he did not know what the "natural flavoring" actually was. I asked if it might be MSG. He was able to assure me that it was not MSG. In the USA, by law, if MSG is used in a food it must be listed on the label I have since learned. But the identity of the natural flavoring I questioned remains a mystery.

Professor Carlos Monteiro, the Brazilian scientist credited with creating the designation ultra-processed food, says they are "often chemically manipulated cheap ingredients" made tasty and attractive by "using combinations of flavors, colors, emulsifiers, thickeners, and other additives." Very often these additives include salt, sugar and preservatives.

What harm can these ultra-processed foods do us? A global study involving almost ten million people and whose findings were published in the British Medical Journal identify 32 ways UPFs can harm our health. Prominent among these are heart disease (number one cause of death in USA and the world) obesity, cancer, high blood pressure and type 2 diabetes. Dr. Chris van Tulleken, author of *Ultra-Processed People* has been quoted: "There is now significant evidence that [UPFs] inflame the gut, disrupt appetite regulation, alter hormone levels and cause myriad other effects which likely increase the risk of disease."

A Reasons for Geographic and Racial Differences in Stroke study that followed 30,000 people over a period of 20 years found that even when you are trying to follow a healthy diet of mostly unprocessed real food, just including a small percentage of UPFs in that healthy diet can increase your risk of cognitive decline and stroke.

UPFs can not only harm physical health, but mental health as well. This global study also found the greater percentage UPFs made of a person's diet, the more likely they were to suffer depression and anxiety. UPFs not only could make you die young, but what years you did live, you likely would be depressed and anxious.

Yet many of these UPFs are marketed as "healthy." And the food industry has designed UPFs to be addictive. Once you begin making them a major part of your diet, you will find it hard to give them up, like smoking or addictive drugs.

When I returned to the USA after years living abroad and growing accustomed to well-prepared real food made from quality ingredients, I found the growing number of UPFs lacked the taste and appetite satisfaction to which I was accustomed. In this respect, I was lucky. I never became addicted to these pseudo-foods. Thank goodness.

I Never Drink Wine Or Other Alcoholic Beverages

The French taught me to love and enjoy good wine. Visits to the UK introduced me to good beers and ale. I always enjoyed these forms of alcohol with food. But then, in the early years of writing the *Chic & Slim* books I began to notice that even expensive wines and craft beers did not agree with me. Particularly I noticed that if I had a small portion of wine with dinner, I did not feel well the next day. When I mentioned the problem with wines in a posting on my website *annebarone.com*, a reader alerted me that even the finest wines had added sugar. I began to suspect that it was the added sugar that was causing my reaction to wine. By my early 60s I gave up drinking alcohol, even with a meal.

What about the non-alcoholic beers and wines now available? I must confess I have not tried either though I understand there are some good taste-like-the-alcoholic version beers. The French, long known for fine wines and champagnes, are making progress in alcohol-free versions of both. In a Guardian article I was interested in a comment by Karima Lounis, a representative of the French no-alcohol brand JNPR, made in Normandy from juniper berries. She pointed out that in France the trend toward alcohol-free beverages was also part of the no-sugar trend. "People don't want sugar in their drinks."

I Never Use Toxic Cleaning Products

The years I was growing up, my mother worked full time. Our family always had a full time nanny/housekeeper. Various "cleaning ladies" came several times a year for major cleaning. Then, after college, the years I lived abroad I always had servants. When, in the early 1970s I returned to live for a while in the USA, I was clueless about household cleaning. I had to do research. I even bought a book on "how to clean everything." It was about this time that concern began to grow about dangers from toxic chemicals in cleaning products.

The information cautioning about chemicals in cleaning products convinced me it could be to the benefit of me and my family to avoid cleaning products with potentially harmful ingredients (especially since my husband and son had serious allergies) and, instead, use natural cleaning products as much as possible. I have done a lot of scrubbing with bicarbonate of soda.

My theory has long been that the fewer toxic chemicals with which my body has to cope, the healthier I will be. And the healthier I am, the better my body can function properly and I will have the health and energy I need to stay slim.

I Never Heat Food In The Microwave In Plastic Containers

I have long been wary of plastic containers. Back in the early 1970s, I read a very convincing article on the dangers of using plastic containers for food storage. Even though Tupperware was the big thing then—and I had acquired several Tupperware items designed for food storage—I thought it best if I used as much glass and CorningWare as possible. Glass jars in which various foods are packaged can be repurposed for refrigerator storage.

If I use plastic wrap, I make sure it does not touch food in the glass or metal container. If for some reason, food must be stored or transported in a plastic container, I use wax paper to wrap foods to minimize contact with the plastic. Given my long avoidance of even storing food in plastic, I am not about to heat anything in the microwave in plastic containers. Some frozen vegetables are packaged in plastic to be steamed. I don't care if they say this is BPA and phthalates free plastic. I am NOT going to heat food in the microwave (or anywhere else) in plastic.

I Never Watch Television

If you read the statistic that only about five percent of American households do not have at least one television, and you try to think of someone you know who lives in such a household, and can't name at least one, here's one: Me.

I gave away my last television about 20 years ago. I have not missed it. Before that I principally used the television for news and for displaying the exercise videos and movies I played on my VCR. Then the Internet came along and I could read the major newspapers of the world on my computer screen and the computer's DVD drive played my exercise DVDs. (These days you must have a stand-alone DVD player or use steaming.)

How do I think that not watching television helps me stay slim? For one thing, I avoid food advertisements that might prompt me to eat ultra-processed foods or just make me hungry and cause me to overeat real, healthy food.

Further, much television programming and advertising is stress-inducing. By not watching television I keep my stress levels down. And stress has been shown to cause weight gain in people who do not overeat. By not watching television I totally avoid political ads which I understand are prevalent in this medium. Additionally unless you have your treadmill or exercise bike set up in front of the television, watching television is most likely a sedentary activity. People who watch a lot of television are often overweight or obese.

What about major events? With a good computer, tablet, and smart phone I don't miss seeing live an inaugural address, damage inflicted by a major disaster, or the funeral of a notable person. And most likely I am able to view those events with blocked advertising.

I Never Participate In Social Media

None of the forerunners to Facebook ever interested me. Kid stuff. When Facebook appeared on the scene, the potential dangers of this platform were to me numerous and obvious. Various smart people wrote and published opinions pointing out the potential negatives of participation. I collected a folder of articles on my computer labeled NOT FACEBOOK.

It was apparent to me that Facebook's founder and head was not smart enough, nor had sufficient life experience to realize to what nefarious uses his creation could be put. Further, I thought him so lacking in morals and ethics that when he did realize the nefarious uses, he would not do anything about them. That has more or less been the case. I have never had a Facebook account.

Twitter, now known as *X*, was a slightly different story. I approached it with caution. At the time that Twitter launched, I had a subscription to *Lynda.com*. The subscription website offered courses in web design, computer use, photography and such. I benefited greatly from the instruction and certainly felt that I got my money's worth. After watching a Twitter tutorial on *Lynda,com*, I thought the platform could be useful to spreading my *Chic & Slim* weight control message. I created a Twitter account. To my horror, I immediately discovered that Twitter had either changed—or had never existed in the way the *Lynda.com* tutorial presented it. I stuck with Twitter for month or so, then abandoned it. One thing that drove me away was that Twitter was beginning to offer targeted ads.

I have a problem with advertising. Those of you who have followed my website *annebarone.com* know there has never been any advertising on that site. My opinion of advertising is that it is designed to encourage people to buy things they don't want or need at prices more than the product or service is worth. (See Apple, whose products and services I buy and love despite their high prices and clever advertising.) I think most of us have more stuff than is good for us. I would not feel comfortable encouraging anyone to buy more. Also I identify food advertising, particularly of ultra-processed foods, as a major cause behind our growing obesity statistics. My non-participation in all social media—especially my non-participation in Facebook, Twitter, Instagram, Snapchat—I am convinced has helped me stay slim.

Social media has been in heavy use for more than a decade now. Evidence is conclusive: Social media can be addictive. And once addicted, this addiction can lead to depression and weight gain.

Sometimes the depression fuels the weight gain. Sometimes weight gain causes the depression. Many anti-depressant medications prescribed to treat depression cause weight gain. How? Antidepressants affect your serotonin that regulates anxiety and mood. But in doing so, serotonin's effect on your brain can also increase your cravings for carbohydrate-rich foods, such as bread, pasta, and desserts.

Several other ways social media can cause weight gain are blatantly obvious. Time hunched over a smartphone or tablet reading "feeds" consumes time that will not be used for healthy exercise. All those photos of delicious food that users post can set off cravings for those foods and can lead to overeating. Photos of others living well and enjoying life can cause you to compare your life with theirs and make you feel that your life is not as good as theirs. These inferior feelings can lead to overconsumption of high calorie comfort foods. No one comforts themselves with a big bowl of steamed green beans.

Stress itself can cause you to gain weight—even when you do not overeat. Social media, especially Facebook and Twitter, is designed to show you information that stresses you in order to keep you "engaged." As Princeton professor of politics and author of *Democracy Rules* Jan-Werner Müller says of Facebook: "For all its sanctimonious talk of "open debate" and "community", its business model is to optimize for outrage; outrage means maximum "engagement" and hence profit." This, Professor Müller calls "incitement capitalism." Why should I become stressed out and ruin my health and appearance so that some people without ethics can get richer?

Furthermore, concern is growing about the erosion of democracy in the tsunami of misinformation that gushes from social media. As Odanga Madung, a data journalist and researcher who views this deterioration from his base in Kenya, put it: "Tech giants have become conflict profiteers. They prioritise profit over preventing harm."

Another problem from excessive social media involves sleep. That blue light from screens can disrupt the natural circadian rhythms of your body causing sleep difficulties. Not enough sleep can lead to numerous health problems, among them heart problems, diabetes and obesity. Because I use a computer to write my books and design my website, I spend a considerable amount of time looking at a screen. If I were to add time spent on social media to these hours of screen each day, this could be a real problem for my health. And for staying slim.

Social media is designed to make you addicted. I have always said "no" to anything addictive. Looking back, I realize saying "no" to social media has helped me stay slim. No doubt my bank account has also benefited by avoiding social media's barrage of pressures to buy, buy, buy.

We have control over our actions, what we choose to do and choose not to do. But in today's world we do not have as much control over stress in our lives. The next chapter deals with how I have prevented unavoidable stress from sabotaging my efforts to stay slim.

The Stress Factor

STRESS. Extreme stress has crowded out hypertension as the "silent killer." In our turbulent times people are so continually and severely stressed that often they are not aware of the fact. Nor aware of the damage stress is doing to their health. Often this damage is weight gain. Stress can cause us to gain weight even if we continue regular exercise and a healthy diet. This damage becomes more likely as we grow older.

When younger, when stressed, our bodies kick in with stress hormones. We recover. Little damage done. But as we age, our body's ability to deal with stress begins to wear out. Like a lot of other abilities.

When we are unable to deal with stress as well as before, our stress can become chronic. This chronic stress accelerates ageing. The process of ageing itself inflicts additional stress. Soon it becomes a vicious cycle.

To help you understand the stress factor and how I prevented stress from causing me to gain weight in a particularly stressful past six years, I will share my story. It is not a happy tale.

Grief is a great stressor. Throughout our lives, we often find ourselves grieving the loss of one who has become essential to our life and happiness. The loss of a spouse, a partner, a friend, or a pet can cause extreme grief.

Shortly after my 74th birthday, one of my cats, my little pastel calico Kiri, was killed under tragic circumstances. I experienced an intense grief brought on not just because in five years Kiri had become important to me, but I felt extreme guilt that I had not been able to prevent her death.

When I shared the news of my loss on the *Chic & Slim* website, cards and emails of consolation and support stabilized me sufficiently that I could begin to search for answers for why I had been so unaware of the danger in our neighborhood. I quickly realized that as a result of a project restoring my old kitchen stove hood, I was exhausted and in pain from the cramped position I had to maintain working under the stove hood on a ladder. This realization prompted a more important question: What could I do to prevent other such tragedies occurring?

In that search, I came upon an article about a recent study done at Purdue University that suggested older women needed even more protein than previously thought. I did a check on how much protein was in my daily diet.

Shock! I thought I was eating such a healthy diet. In truth, I was not getting even a third of my daily protein needs. No wonder my body and brain were not functioning well.

I set out to add more protein to my diet. In itself this was a good idea. But the manner in which I went about it caused serious problems. First, I broke one of my own major rules for changes in eating habits. Why did I not remember dietary changes must be made gradually?

Unfortunately when stressed you often do not think as clearly as in normal times. People under stress often make decisions not in their best interest. I certainly did.

The results of immediately switching from a fourth cup of homemade plain yogurt a day to one cup of commercial Greek yogurt, adding soy isolate protein powder, increasing consumption of beans, lentils, and other high protein plants as well as lean protein in fish and chicken resulted in drastic digestive problems. Within a month I was having serious issues with bloating and noisy flatulence. Neither are chic. As a result, I basically became a housebound recluse while I tried one, then another techniques and products and feverishly searched for remedies when those tried did not work.

I kept food journals. I tried every suggestion medical science offered for preventing and treating intestinal gas. I could have financed a vacation in the Caribbean on what I spent on digestive enzymes, probiotics, prebiotics, and anti-gas pills. I experimented with Monash University's FODMAPS Diet. I investigated whether I was lactose or gluten intolerant. Then, histamine intolerant. I made sure I was not swallowing air when I ate. Nothing helped.

Then on the 31st of March 2019, the bottom fell out. Literally. Just hours before the dawn of April Fool's Day, I suffered a pelvic floor prolapse. But it was not a joke. And I had extreme difficulty dealing with the reality of it. For three days I was in COMPLETE and TOTAL DENIAL.

This was not happening, I told myself. I was Anne Barone. I was in good health. I was not overweight. I ate good nutrition. I exercised. One of my internal organs did not slide out of my lower region like a half-laid egg. This was temporary, my denying self insisted. The condition would clear up. My bladder would retreat back inside where it was supposed to be. Of course, pelvic prolapse does not "clear up" by itself.

When my 72 hours of denial wore out, I began to deal with the situation rationally. What surprised me most was that I had written two books on certain age women and in my research, I had never found pelvic floor prolapse mentioned. The only thing I knew about prolapse was that in the last days of completing *Toujours 2*, I had a phone call from a good friend. She told me that she had surgery for pelvic prolapse. I had never heard of the condition and had the impression from our phone conversation that it was uncommon. Actually it was at that time the condition of about one-fourth the adult women in the USA.

In any case, my friend's surgery had gone badly. As a result she had been hospitalized for two months but was now finally home from the hospital. Sadly she never recovered from the surgery and died just a little over a year later. One thing I decided from my friend's tragic experience: corrective surgery was definitively out.

I did a check on the Mayo Clinic website, and for prolapse, they recommended Kegel exercises to strengthen the pelvic floor. I found a helpful instructional video on the website of the Canadian women's magazine *Chatelaine*. I began doing three sessions of Kegel's daily: 20 reps on waking, 20 mid-day and 20 at bedtime. Sometimes my bladder protruded. Part of the time it was back inside. For that, I began calling my bladder Yoyo. Life went on.

The Mayo Clinic article on prolapse had mentioned a pessary to hold the bladder inside. But the reports by women who used them said they were uncomfortable and with a tendency to fall out. Oh dear!

I was still trying to deal with the grief and guilt as a result of Kiri's death. The noisy flatulence was still a problem. But I continued to keep a food diary and try various methods and products to help with the bloating and noisy gas.

Prolapse requires modification to activities. I had to be careful of lifting. Nothing more than 10 pounds. Breathe out as I lifted. I also had to be careful mowing. The strain my push mower put on my pelvic muscles had the potential to make my prolapse problem worse. I had not yet become incontinent, but I was getting hints that I might reach that point if I were not extremely careful.

By the end of September with my vigorous exercise winding down, I needed to look at exercise options for the months I would not be walking or mowing. The first thing I noted was that at that time there was not a great deal of information about exercise with prolapse on American websites. Was the fact that prolapse in the USA was more common in older women who were not as likely to be doing Pilates and working out at the gym? Thirty-seven percent of American women with prolapse were 60 to 79. More than half were 80 and older. The most information on prolapse I found (in English at least) was from the Australian national health service and related organizations. Understandable when I read that one in three adult women in Australia had suffered prolapse. In Australia, at least, prolapse was not so much an "old lady problem."

When I began studying the Australian articles and videos, I soon saw that my pre-prolapse exercise program required much modification. A number of exercises I had been doing were prohibited with prolapse. Fortunately modifications had been worked out. For instance, with prolapse, you were advised against doing the plank. But there was a modified plank that could be substituted. Some yoga poses were allowed. A number not.

The woman who seemed to have captured the market for exercising with prolapse was an Australian Michelle Kenway. I bought her video and book. But I had three basic problems with Michelle Kenway's video. In all the exercise videos I had previously used the exercises were done barefoot. Michelle Kenway wore clunky, to me extremely unchic, exercise shoes. Second, I had difficulty understanding her Australian accent and the different terminology she used for bodily functions. Third, her exercises seemed too anemic and they did not do the job that my previous exercise program did. Her exercises to tone the abdomen were nothing on the order of the Pilates I had done several decades. After a couple of months I never used the video again. Too, with prolapse, you are only allowed to work out on a treadmill if it is flat. My treadmill was incline-only. The recommendation was that an exercise bike was better for prolapse than a treadmill. I might have bought an exercise bicycle sooner, but then a new and more potent stressor arrived in my life.

From the time of Kiri's death, I had seen that each new serious stress in my life caused a physical problem. The gas/digestive problems onset soon after her death. The pelvic prolapse, the day the bladder descended was the immediately following a very stressful trip back to the town in which I had been born and grew up. But now, not long after the beginning of 2020, we had the first hints of the pandemic that would be declared. Soon Covid-19 as it was designated, would bring lockdowns, social distancing, school closings, masks, hand sanitizers, and the Great Toilet Tissue Shortage. Stress piled upon stress.

For me there were two additional stress elements of Covid. I knew from living in parts of the world with extreme health risks that I had better than average resistance to bacterial infections.

But I had little resistance to viral infections. Covid was a virus. And I was 75, in that age range most vulnerable to death from Covid for which there was (at that time) no vaccine. Medications doctors were trying were not that effective. People were dying.

I decided my best defense against Covid (and severe illness, possibly death) was to stay at home. I had already had more than a year of being almost housebound with the noisy gas problem. I ventured out only to shop for groceries. Now, with Covid I could fill much of my needs ordering online. The only problem I could see was fresh produce. But it was spring and growing in my garden I had poke as an asparagus/greens substitute and wild violet leaves as spinach substitute. My nutrition would not be as good as before and that would make me more vulnerable to the virus. But that seemed the best I could do. In hindsight, my decision to put myself in severe lockdown seems unnecessarily restrictive. On the other hand, I am still here.

At least Covid distracted me from the feeling of grief and guilt for my cat's death I was still suffering. And, despite my age and vulnerability to viruses, I had one thing in my favor, I was not overweight. As Covid claimed its first victims, the media featured articles about these people, including photos. I immediately noticed that most were obese.

A lot of people gained weight during the Covid pandemic. I did not. Why? Given the stress I was already suffering when the pandemic was declared in early March 2020, how was I able to avoid putting on extra pounds?

Beyond stress's negative effects on weight gain, factors that caused many to gain weight during the pandemic was that lockdown interrupted regular exercise programs (could not go to the gym, in some cities could not take walks). Work from home gave many more opportunities for snacking, shopping interruptions prevented buying fresh produce, comfort foods were too often sugary and ultra-processed foods. New interest revived in home cooking and people ate what they cooked.

Teachers of genre fiction often instruct their students to begin the story "at the moment that made the difference." At the point when something happens to the protagonist that challenges their self definition of who they are.

If this were a novel instead of a book about how I lost weight and stayed slim 55 years, I would have begun the book with my prolapse. In a novel, I, already grieving and suffering from a health condition that kept me housebound, would have been so thrown off balance by the prolapse that I would have gained a lot of weight and then struggled to take it off.

That did not happen.

The chief thing that sees me through all sorts of stressful situations without gaining weight is that having succeeded in losing weight and staying slim these 55 years, has given me confidence that I can deal with anything that comes my way. It may take some time, as it has with those gassy digestive problems, but eventually I solve the problem.

I am happy to say as I am doing the final edit of this book, I have those noisy gas problems under control. In part it was a question of coming to terms with the grief and guilt from my cat's tragic death. Combined with recovering from problems I inflicted on myself with my initial too radical change in diet in my initial response to those problems. And with coming to the understanding of the roll my pelvic prolapse was playing in the digestive problems.

Yet, in hindsight, my digestive problems were a blessing in disguise. I was keeping a food diary as a means of identifying what was causing the excessive flatulence. This record made me aware of exactly what I was eating, and when, and the amounts. It kept me eating a healthy diet rather than "comfort foods" to which many stressed people turn. Actually, one recommendation for successfully dealing with stress is eating a healthy diet. Broccoli, sweet potatoes, black-eyed peas, almonds, spinach, eggs, and beets all contain vitamins and minerals that help our bodies and brains cope with stress.

Another recommendation for dealing with stress is exercise. This works in an interesting way. Our bodies are designed for dealing with stress, just not the sorts of stress most people suffer in the present time.

Rather it was designed for a time when you might be out in the forest gathering herbs for cooking and you look up and see a woolly mammoth charging, or your enemy brandishing a club advancing to whack you in the head.

Sensing danger, our pituitary glands shoot out adrenaline and cortisol. Glucose is there for energy. These hormones give us the energy to outrun the woolly mammoth or our enemy. Once back in the safety of our hut, danger is over and our bodies stop producing the hormones that came to our aid. In running to escape the danger, we have burned up the glucose.

But today our stresses are more likely micro-stressors. For example, co-worker makes a tacky comment, the customer service rep is being unnecessary dense, the dog threw up on the rug five minutes before guests arrive. Or macro-stressors: you can't find a nursing home you can afford for your elderly father, you loose your job in a company downsizing, you see expenses continually rising beyond your income. These stresses remain and your body keeps producing those stress hormones. And the glucose, because it is not burned up instead turns to fat. And worse, the fat this glucose produces settles around your middle as unsightly belly fat.

But exercise can help bring those stress hormones back to normal. All through these stressful years, I have made sure that I stayed with my exercise program even though the prolapse required substantial changes. In fact, the more stressed I feel, the higher priority I give exercise in my daily routine.

Some people thrive in chaos. Not me. A cluttered house, especially one that also needs the attention of vacuum, mop, and dust cloth makes it difficult for me to think and function well. Cleaning and organizing my living space gives me a sense of control that can go a long way toward relieving stress.

We can't prevent stress. But we can deal with it so it will not bring harm to our minds and bodies, especially the harm of excess weight which, in turn, puts us at risk of a host of serious diseases.

But stress and the way a person deals with stress is unique to every individual. Just as with losing weight and staying slim, you have to look at the best medical science and then use what works for you and your lifestyle. And it helps if you have understanding friends who give you consolation and support. I am so thankful for my *Chic & Slim* Baronettes.

My focus of the past half-century has been staying slim. But beginning a few years ago, new challenges presented themselves as my natural process of ageing kicked in. The next chapter discusses ways to cope with the changes that ageing brings.

Coping With Natural Ageing

WHAT HAPPENS TO OUR BODIES as we age is not pretty. Parts you want to keep flat bulge out. Parts you want to keep rounded go flat. Some parts do not function often enough. Some parts function too frequently. Sarcopenia. Osteoporosis. Hearing Loss. Gingivitis. Age Spots. Cataracts. Macular Degeneration. Cognitive Decline. Dementia. When you were younger, you didn't have to worry about this stuff. But as you age, it is a different matter. Prevention, or at least delaying progression of these problems, can eat up a lot of time and energy. Ageing well demands fortitude and stamina. Ageing is not for the faint-hearted.

All and all, at 80, as far as ageing goes, I am not doing badly. No, I cannot do the splits like that 84-year-old fitness instructor in the UK. Nor do I win marathons like the 100-year-old Japanese runner. But I can do all the things I need to do for a satisfying and productive life. Health problems I do have are more inconvenient than disabling. They are manageable.

I have been fortunate in my genetic inheritance. My mother and both my grandmothers lived to healthy old ages. My mother and paternal grandmother lived to 93. My maternal grandmother lived to 99. Beyond genetics, I benefited from observing my mother and maternal grandmother's devotion to exercise and meaningful work. Both important for successful ageing.

Those of you who follow my website *annebarone.com* and have seen my photos there through the decades know that the years have not taken too great a toll on my appearance. The oily skin that has plagued me with breakouts since puberty now has the benefit of resisting wrinkles. Though I have been careful about skin care and protection from the sun—at least in the last decade or so.

Graying

But only in the last year have I begun to see some silvering in my hair. This delayed graying is not the result of anything I have done. (Though you can read all sorts of advice on the Internet for preventing hair turning gray.) My delayed graying is purely genetic. Neither my mother nor maternal grandmother's hair began to gray until they were in their 80s. Instead, about age 50 our medium brown hair turns black. Very black. Not flattering with our skin tone.

My grandmother never did more than allow a hairdresser to apply a rinse that treated the ugly yellow streaks (like a bad highlighting with peroxide) that appeared in her black hair at the beginning of the graying process. But she wore her hair that she never cut in her lifetime braided and coiled into a bun at the nape of her neck. The streaks were not as noticeable as they might have been in another hairstyle. When my mother's blackening hair became more and more unflattering, her hairdresser convinced her to become a blonde. And that took care of that problem.

I was already highlighting my hair when my hair began its transition to black. Eventually I went from only highlighting to full head coloring, then, highlighting over the haircolor using a technique I learned from an article I read written by a New York colorist.

At whatever age a woman's hair grays, today there are excellent hair coloring products and good colorists to give you whatever color and shade you want. Also, in recent years, natural gray hair for women has become not only acceptable, but, for many, desirable. Especially since it does away with the necessity and expense of coloring sessions. And for many women it is more flattering than colored hair. Though some find subtle lowlights in their white or gray hair the chicest compromise between gray and full head color.

Sarcopenia

Sarcopenia is the fancy medical name a doctor coined for the ageing process in which particularly the thigh and abdominal muscles vanish and fat takes the muscles' place. Some studies have found that increasing protein intake, particularly animal protein, combined with resistance exercise can counteract sarcopenia. Other studies found that increased protein and resistance exercise do not help.

Since the amount of additional protein and exercise was substantial and, in any case, not guaranteeing results, I have found another solution. I always had powerhouse thighs on my short legs. Even though the lost muscle mass has resulted in flabby skin, I find that wearing a good pair of leggings with plenty of spandex I have the best-looking legs I've ever had.

Posture And Flexibility

Maintaining good posture is a constant battle that I am not always winning. Two activities at which I spend a great deal of my time: working at a computer and gardening, are disastrous for my posture. To counter the always-incipient dowager's hump trying to establish itself on my back, I regularly work out with one of *Aging Backwards* author Miranda Esmonde-White's posture videos.

And in my house I have many mirrors. No vanity here. Those mirrors provide a constant check on my posture and a reminder as Miranda Esmonde-White admonishes: "Shoulder blades in your back pockets." A reminder to pull my shoulders back and down.

I am glad my doctor insisted that I take hormone replacement therapy following my hysterectomy. Through the almost ninety years it has been available, HRT has proven to be one of the best preventive treatments for osteoporosis, that condition in which the bones become fragile and more vulnerable to fracture.

In addition to the HRT, my doctor prescribed calcium and magnesium supplementation. And I make sure my diet includes a lot of leafy greens and a reasonable amount of dairy. Walking, a major part of my exercise program, provides that weight bearing exercise that helps keep bones strong.

Breasts

Unfortunately, in the breast department, I neglected any sort of preventative measures against flattening. And I mean flat. Which has led me to consider the possibility that the reason some women gain weight in their later years is that fat keeps their breasts shapely.

But since I prefer the health benefits of staying slim, I have rejected that solution. But my flattened breasts have thrown my proportions out of balance. My torso has become a triangle, not an hourglass. My solution is to switch to mastectomy bras in which I can insert prostheses pads. It took some experimentation to get the combination right. And algebra. If the breast tissue is X, and the pad is Y, what size mastectomy bra cup is necessary to accommodate the two and look natural? Adjusting to wearing the pads took a while, but now I hardly notice them.

Of course, another solution many women choose for the changes ageing makes to their breasts is breast augmentation surgery. But I waited so long that, by the time the flattening came a couple of years ago, I was at an age where any cosmetic surgery carries definite risks. I decided against surgical augmentation on the grounds that I wanted a classier obituary than: She died having a boob job.

Teeth And Gums

It is hard to eat a healthy diet if you have teeth and gum problems. Gingivitis is another of those things you have to watch out for as you age. If your gums become inflamed, you do not want to let it get out of hand. That little gingivitis infection in your gum untreated can worsen into periodontitis. Then, a weakened jaw. Then your teeth might fall out. Good grief!

In recent years dentists have been advising us that we need to use an alcohol-free mouthwash because the alcohol-based versions, though effective against gingivitis, can reduce saliva production and cause dry mouth. Okay. So after decades of using Listerine, the original, I tried an alcohol-free version. Yuck. I couldn't tolerate the sweet taste from all the sugar (by various other names, of course) in the mouthwashes. Back to the original Listerine.

For occasional mouth sores, an OTC peroxide-based rinse is useful. If that isn't clearing up the problem fast enough to suit me, my dental hygienist recommended an alcohol-free antimicrobial oral rinse that is anticavity, antihypersensitiity, antigingivitis. Basically a fluoride rinse with some glycerin. Kind of pricey, but it works well and quickly.

Eyes And Vision

For the past decade I have had small cataracts in my eyes. At my last eye checkup when the doctor tried to talk to me about cataract surgery, I told him that I would get a seeing-eye dog before I would have those cataracts removed.

I am totally terrified of anyone cutting on my eyes. As it is, I am getting along quite well with toric multifocal contact lenses. For long sessions at the computer or reading as for the research and writing of this book, I have progressive bifocals optimized for the computer.

As extra insurance I have long practiced prevention techniques for cataracts: Wear sunglasses that give protection from UVA and UVB rays, wear a sunhat for even greater protection, keep watch on blood sugar, limit alcohol, and eat a diet with nutrients that promote eye health, especially vitamin C and vitamin E.

So far examinations have found no signs of macular degeneration in my eyes. About the time I met my good friend Betty in Corpus Christi, she had just been diagnosed with this age-related eye disease. Her ophthalmologist told her to eat spinach four times a week. She did this without fail. Though there was no improvement neither did the problem worsen until she was in her early 90s. Those 30 years ago I began to regularly eat spinach weekly. And more often since I really like spinach. Later I began supplements based on the National Eye Institute's AREDS 2 study.

The AREDS 2 study (Age-Related Eye Disease Study 2) refined the Eye Institutes's original definition of what nutrients were effective against macular degeneration and promoted eye health. Vitamin C 500 mg, vitamin E 400 IU, copper 2 mg, zinc 22 mg, lutein 10 mg, zeaxanthin 2 mg daily.

A number of companies make a combo pill combining these nutrients. But I have my reservations about supplements that combine more than one nutrient (this based on research that shows that taking some nutrients at the same time as another hinders the absorptions of one or the other. Or all.) So I meet my requirements with single nutrient supplements. And I still eat my spinach and my kale and my raw carrots.

Even if one takes supplements for eye health, diet is still vitally important in keeping eyes healthy. Additionally, recent medical studies have found a direct relationship between the consumption of red meat as well as processed meats and the increased the risk of age-related eye disease. Oh, dear. At times it seems as if the general food rule for good health in ageing is: If it tastes good, spit it out.

Hearing

My hearing has always been excellent, and I have been very careful to avoid damage to that good hearing. Not only do I religiously wear earplugs when using my noisy lawn equipment, but also when I use my blender or vacuum. Both household appliances are loud and potentially damaging to my hearing.

If I do begin to notice hearing loss, these days there have been great advances in hearing aids both in price and technology. Just as I am completing this book, the FDA, the US Food and Drug Administration, has approved Apple's AirPods Pro 2 ear buds for use as a hearing aid for those with mild to moderate hearing loss. That is an estimated 30 million American adults, a good portion of whom do not use any sort of hearing aid because of cost, frustration with quality of sound reproduction of existing devices and stigma of wearing a hearing aid.

Since I have lived entirely within the Apple ecosystem since my first computer, these ear buds would be a natural first step for me should I begin to experience hearing loss. In any case I have vowed that even if I become deaf as a post, I will not constantly ask people to repeat. Much of what people say these days is probably better not understood anyway.

Cognitive Function And Dementia

When my mother was in her late 80s, I overheard one of my brothers telling a cousin: "Momma can't remember what she had for breakfast. But she can tell you everybody who came to Christmas dinner in 1962." Such is often the reality of the ageing brain. But there are things we can do to prevent becoming someone who remembers a holiday dinner guest list decades previously better than breakfast that morning.

Like the other parts of our bodies, our brains require exercise to function well. This is true all our lives, but it is especially important when natural cognitive decline sets. Of course I get a lot of brain exercise writing books as well as writing articles for the *annebarone.com* website. Plus every couple of years for one reason or another I have to learn a new operating system for my computer, plus a new software program for creating the website, yet another for designing the books, print and ebook.

Older people are constantly being told they must do crossword puzzles to keep their brains from turning to mush. I have enough brain exercise working with words I don't need crossword puzzles. But as part of keeping my brain working well as long as possible,

I decided what I needed was brain exercise involving numbers.

I tried the most highly recommended number game Sudoku. Numbers it was, but Sudoku and I did not click. The game reminded me of a Rubik's Cube with which I did not "click" either. I play FreeCell which has the blessing of The Association of Mature American Citizens. For the last 10 or so years, I have played two games per day, one mid-day, the second in the evening. Then there is the numbers exercise in bookkeeping for my book business. And the great fun each year doing my federal income taxes.

But it isn't just the brain exercises that are important in preventing cognitive decline. Medical research studying prevention and treatment of dementia is finding that physical exercise is equally, if not more, necessary. The concern about my cognitive function keeps me walking and riding my exercise bike and working out with my exercise videos when I would really prefer to just sit and sip tea and read a good book.

Having a healthy brain resistant to cognitive decline, like staying slim, depends to a great extent on what you eat—and what you do not eat.

I found it reassuring when I learned that the Mediterranean style of eating was recommended for brain health since that is the general style of eating that I have followed for decades. Also recommended is the DASH (Dietary Approaches to Stop Hypertension) diet. DASH, however, is too restrictive for me. No added salt to food ever! Plus the DASH diet demands a first two weeks of "resetting the metabolism" in which no fruit or grains are eaten. Two weeks with no fresh fruit and no bread? Not possible.

In any case, one thing I have learned in more than 55 years of staying slim is that the human body does not like radical change.

It will fight against it. You try to make major changes too quickly and likely you will be miserable. And unsuccessful. Better to make changes gradually so you will have a greater chance of making those positive dietary changes permanent.

But is there any diet better than the Mediterranean or DASH diets at preventing cognitive decline?

A few years ago Dr. Martha Clare Morris and colleagues at Rush University Medical Center along with the Harvard Chan School of Public Health created a diet designed to give protection against dementia and cognitive deterioration. What they came up with was the MIND Diet, the Mediterranean-DASH Diet Intervention for Neurodegenerative Delay. The MIND diet recommends specific categories of "brain healthy" foods and five unhealthy categories to limit or exclude.

When I did the questionnaire for the MIND diet, I did not do as well as I had on the questionnaire for the Harvard alternative healthy eating index (AHEI) that I wrote about previously in this book.

I did meet the MIND requirements: 3 servings a day for whole grains, 1 per day of vegetables not leafy green and 6 per week of leafy green. In fact, I eat more whole grains and veggies than required. I also meet the requirement for 5 servings per week of nuts, 4 per week of beans, 2 per week of berries and poultry and at least fish once a week. I actually eat fish several meals during a week. And I do use extra virgin olive oil as the principal fat in my diet.

But my downfall in the MIND diet's limited or excluded list was cheese. I eat a small serving of cheese almost every day. (Blame the French.) The MIND diet only allows one serving of cheese per week. Per week! Though as anyone who shops in American supermarkets and who has any experience with the kind of cheese sold in cheese shops in other parts of the world knows that much of what is sold as cheese in the USA is what I call pseudo-cheese. Sort of like cheese, but not really cheese as it has been known for centuries. Quite a number of those pseudo-cheeses meet the definition for ultra-processed food.

For the most part, the cheeses I eat are goat milk and sheep milk cheeses imported from Spain, Italy and France. I order them from a cheese importer in New York. The MIND diet's prohibition on cheese is based on cheese's fat and sodium content. But the MIND diet does acknowledge that goat milk and sheep milk cheeses are generally lower in sodium and fat than cow's milk cheeses. I also find them easier to digest. Not to mention that I really prefer the strong, tangy tastes of these cheeses. At present I am particularly enjoying a Spanish *queso de cabra* made from the milk of a heritage herd of Payoya Andalusian goats.

So I don't think I am doing my brain too much damage eating a little cheese most days. Especially since I more than meet the MIND requirements for limiting sweets, red meat, fried food and butter.

Sleep

In addition to exercise for both brain and body and a brain-healthy diet, good sleep is necessary to prevent cognitive decline. As I have written on the website, adequate sleep has been a big problem for me because a combination of noisy neighbors and my cat who had taken to waking me every two hours or so during the night. Solving (partially) this problem took some active discipline with water in a spray bottle and a lot of yelling (at the cat, not the neighbors). Now most nights I am able to sleep from the time the neighbors settle down until around 5 AM when Miss Cat starts yowling. I hope for further progress.

Recall

One thing I have to accept is that eventually, despite my prevention efforts, I may have the problem remembering where I put things and having to hunt. One of the most sensible pieces of advice for dealing with this problem is decluttering.

Mostly known for her Regency romances, the writer Georgette Heyer wrote nine mystery novels that number among my favorites principally because of their humor. In her 1935 *Death in the Stocks* she has fun with a character, a middle-aged lawyer who has an extremely cluttered desk and office. Consequently he is continually fussily hunting what he needs.

Remembering Miss Heyer's lawyer I am attempting to get rid of everything non-essential so that when I need the essentials, I will have a better chance of spotting them if they are not lost among a morass of stuff.

Bones And Falls

No matter how healthy your diet and the quality of your exercise, ageing is going to produce brittling of the bones. Making it more likely that a fall might cause fractures. So the older I become the more important it is that I do not fall.

My grandmother's house had high steps from her screened back porch down to a concrete areaway. Grandmother, even as the years accumulated and she was not as steady on her feet as she had been, continued to do everything at breakneck speed. Too often she charged out her back porch door and took a tumble down to the concrete. Miraculously she never broke any bones in these falls. But I would often stop by her house on my way home from school and find her with a new set of purpling bruises.

Most of us will not just bounce and bruise the way my grandmother did. Too often we will break bones or injure our heads. And broken bones and head injuries will complicate our lives. Injuries also may make it impossible to exercise properly, or prepare our own meals, or care for our homes (cleaners are scarce and expensive), do the things necessary for our quality of life. We may have to wear casts or slings or walk on crutches. Casts and slings and crutches rarely add to chic.

As for preventing falls, you don't have to look far for advice on fall prevention. Dozens of sources will advise on a multitude of exercises and techniques including instructions for falling so you will do yourself the least amount of damage. Balance is important. Part of the posture improvement video I use has a balance segment where you stand on one foot and then the other writing the alphabet in the air with the elevated foot. I am a realist. I always stand close enough to something I can grab if I start to fall. I also clear my exercise area so if I do fall, I won't do myself too much damage.

Walking on uneven ground is also good for maintaining your sense of balance. Beyond balance is keeping your house free of things you could trip over or slip on. If you spill something on the floor, wipe it up. Immediately. Watch out for electrical cords.

My cousin told me that I should always take my cellphone into the bathroom with me and put it on the floor. So, if I fall and can't get up, the phone will be down there where I can reach it and call for help. Yes, if I haven't stepped on and demolished that $500 iPhone in the meantime.

In any case, proper footwear is good prevention against falls. You can continue to look chic, but you must choose shoes that are practical as well as chic. Furthermore, if you have long been devoted to ultra high heels, at some point in your advancing years, you may need to think about more moderate heel height. I am watching with interest to see to what age a couple of celebrities now in their 70s continue to trot around in five-inch heels.

Energy

Ageing is exhausting. It takes stamina to cope with all the changes your body is making that deplete your energy. Back in my fatty days I always seemed to have plenty of energy. Was I just running on carbs? No. Though I ate too much cake, pie, cookies, candy and other sugary foods, otherwise I ate a healthy diet with quality protein, whole grains, and lots of homegrown fruits and vegetables.

It was in my mid-20s after I lost those 55 pounds that I began to have problems with low energy. Despite the doctor-prescribed iron pills and a healthy diet with lots of iron-rich food, I always seemed to stay borderline anemic. Consequently energy was a problem. This, however, was not a result of my weight loss, but rather my problematic gynecological system. From puberty I had always had horrendously painful menstrual periods. Labor without anesthesia when my son was born was a picnic compared what I had gone through monthly for years.

In hindsight, after my hysterectomy at age 43, it became obvious that my problems with energy beginning in my mid-20s had been caused by my gynecological system. Surgery and the hormone replacement therapy that began even before I was out from under the anesthesia gave me a new, more energetic life.

I deeply regretted that I had put off having the operation until it became an emergency. I realized that I had suffered unnecessarily and forfeited more than a decade of my life to pain and emotional upsets.

With my new energy, I relocated to the Texas Gulf Coast. I began writing the *Chic & Slim* series of books. I enjoyed life. At 63, two decades after my hysterectomy, I began taking myself gradually off my replacement hormones and did not notice any decrease in energy until I was almost 70. The summer of 2012 we had an outbreak of West Nile Virus here in Texas. Official statistics state 1,868 reported cases. Heaven only knows how many of us had this miserable neuroinvasive disease who never reported it. The Dallas/Fort Worth area had 48% of West Nile reported cases. And, as the mosquitoes swarm, I live relatively near Dallas/Fort Worth.

The symptoms of West Nile are much those of the flu. Before I realized the danger I had been bitten by mosquitoes and was suffering all the symptoms. I had lived in West Africa in my 20s and had nursed friends though Denge Fever, another mosquito-borne virus with similar symptoms as West Nile. Treatment for both require staying hydrated, pain-relievers and lots of rest until you finally recover. Assuming you recover.

So for most of the month of June I managed little more than to keep myself and the cats fed and do minimal housework. One chore, rest, another chore, rest . . . Writing articles for the *Chic & Slim* website was out of the question. My brain could barely handle light reading. But when I did recover, I was back to my previous energy level. This continued until that summer I was so devastated by grief and guilt over the tragic death of my little cat. But I had already been suffering from very low energy several weeks before Kiri's death.

This extreme fatigue I chalked up to an intensive four-day restoration project on the old 1920s range hood in which I had to work in a contorted position and breathed a lot of stripping chemical fumes.

As I wrote earlier in this book, the stress from the grief and guilt I felt over my cat's death further depleted my already low energy. This prompted me to search for a better explanation for my fatigue than the range hood restoration work. The analysis of how much protein I was eating prompted me to take some actions that caused severe digestive problems. One step forward and two steps back. Then came the Covid pandemic. Additionally, as I progressed into my late 70s, ageing began to be a stronger factor in my decreasing energy levels. The unhappy fact is that naturally our energy declines as we age. We lose muscle mass and strength and we become less flexible. We tire more from less exertion.

But what could I do to slow this natural process? When I first researched "keeping energy levels high in older adults" I was disappointed to find I had little room for improvement. I was already doing those things suggested. I ate a healthy diet, real whole foods with lots of protein and I was sure to include animal protein that older people's bodies use best. I drank green tea, took vitamin B-12 and vitamin D-3 supplements, as well as magnesium. I kept myself well hydrated.

As for the uninterrupted sleep, I had made definite improvement in this area. I faithfully did my aerobic and stretching exercises within the limits put on exercise by my pelvic prolapse. All that and I still did not have the energy level I wanted and needed to cope with my current lifestyle writing and running my publishing business and taking care of my house and large garden. So what else could I do?

After honest reflection, I knew I was unlikely to increase my energy level substantially further. I am, after all, 80. So I decided the obvious solution was simply to do less with the amount of energy I have.

I keep a card I use as a bookmark on which I have written: "Simplicity—the art of maximizing the amount of work not done—is essential." It is one of the principles of the Agile Manifesto for software development, but nonetheless useful for almost anything you do.

The point is to eliminate waste—in time, energy, materials. But not to eliminate so much that you don't accomplish your goal. So how in practical terms do I get the most from the amount of energy I have by maximizing the amount of work that I do not do? What am I doing now that I can eliminate and still live a satisfying, healthy lifestyle?

The obvious first step in my effort to maximize the amount of work not done was to make a time analysis. Analyzing how you spend your time, like keeping a food diary of what you eat, is only useful if you are brutally honest and exact. The goal of my time analysis was to identify what activities could be done more efficiently—and which might be totally eliminated.

Surprisingly, the first discovery I made was that I my poorly designed plastic dish drainer was wasting a lot of my time with things falling over, falling out, not draining properly. Sounds small. But I do not have a dishwasher and cook all my meals from scratch. That makes for a lot of hand dishwashing. And remember, if you can save five minutes a day 365 days a year, that adds up to more than 30 hours. My new larger, better-designed stainless steel dish drainer will save me more than 30 hours.

A bigger timesaver, and certainly bigger energy saver, is to take out of most of those privet shrubs I have planted since I bought this property.

Privet is the shrub of choice for my Tudoresque house, and I have become very good at growing, shaping and trimming the shrub. My privet enhanced my property and made for great photos on the *Chic & Slim* website. But to keep all my privet shrubs properly shaped requires a lot of time and effort. Untrimmed privet gives the property an unkept appearance. I tried hiring someone to do the trimming, and for the considerable money dispensed, my privet bushes were butchered. "They'll grow back, Ma'am" was the sheepish response to my complaint. Taking out the privet and replacing it with shrubs that do not require such frequent trimming will make for a big savings in time and energy. Those electric hedge trimmers are heavy.

Since the publication of the first *Chic & Slim* book in 1997, my life has been a continual series of interruptions to projects that have to be temporarily abandoned for one reason or another. Moves. Illness. Another project takes priority. Especially book and website design projects suffered interruption. Of course, these interruptions sometimes as much as doubled the time it took to complete the project. This is not an efficient way to work. Or live. And right now I have a superfluity of partially-completed projects that weigh on me like a three-stand necklace of bricks.

So a decision: "Come hell or high water," as the expression goes, I will not begin any new projects until my numerous partially completed projects, rated by priority, are finished. Or abandoned. Or hired out— if I can find someone who can do the work (a) better than I can do it myself (b) finish the job in a reasonable amount of time and (c) do the work at a price I can afford. At the top of my list is finishing the interior painting of my house. And I do know of a team of house painters whose interior wall and trim painting is an absolute work of art with NO spills or mess. But they charge about $3000 a room. Alas.

Then the obvious question: why don't I just downsize like so many people do? Sell this half-acre property and its 95-year-old house and garage with apartment all needing constant repairs, trees and shrubs that need trimming, flower beds that require weeding, and move to a condo as did when I sold my house and moved to the Texas Gulf Coast and began writing the *Chic & Slim* books? There I did not even have to take trash to the dumpster. Plus the place had an Olympic-sized pool.

I have not totally ruled out that possibility. But not yet. A lot of people I know who downsized regretted it. Deeply. At this point in my life, I think I also would regret that move.

One reason I put such effort into care of my body and brain is so that I can continue to live in this place that I have spent the past decade and a half creating as my own *Provence-sur-la-Prairie*. I need my solitude, my garden with my trees, and shrubs and flowers, my birds and squirrels and possum. Though, given the expensive damage this most recent family of raccoons have done, I can do without those critters.

In any case, mine is an elder-friendly house. The previous owner lived here almost forty years, the last decade and a half she suffered Parkinson's and died here at age 89. I have been making additional modifications for safety and convenience. These days even many centenarians are comfortably living alone.

As for maximizing the amount of work not done on my writing, this is my last full length book, certainly the last to appear in print as well as ebook format. The trend in information consumption is for shorter. Further publications will be on the *annebarone.com* website or in other digital formats.

Those things I have just discussed are a start. And I am sure that, just as I was inspired by chic French women's techniques to create my own system to lose weight and stay slim, that I can discover sufficient ideas to maximize my amount of work not done and have sufficient energy to cope well with the natural changes my body and mind are making.

Living Well

I DEDICATED THIS BOOK to my maternal grandmother Besse and to her sister, my great aunt Sudie. Though they were very different, each provided me a wonderful role model for successful ageing. And it was Great Aunt Sudie who introduced me to the idea that French women had good advice for successful living—and for chic and staying slim.

Some of you may have been surprised by my enthusiasm for the new weight loss medications. Especially since during my weight loss and maintenance of that loss I have not used any medical assistance.

But throughout these more than 55 years of staying slim I have observed many women struggling with their weight. I have had many conversations with them about their struggles. Early on it became apparent to me that many people, both men and women, who had problems with weight-maintenance did not have the determination, the self-discipline and the self-confidence of success that I possess.

And sadly some lacked another necessary ingredient for a maintaining a normal body weight: the income for, and access to, healthy food.

My system worked for me, and it has worked for others as well. But I knew even as I was writing the first *Chic & Slim* book that it would take a weight loss "silver bullet," a medical solution, to help many of the overweight and certainly the excessively obese.

As I said in the introduction of this book, I am very interested in observing what the availability of these weight loss medications—and other better and less expensive ones surely to come—have on our lives and lifestyles. But I certainly do not see a future in which everyone is a healthy weight. Puritanical voices are already crying loudly that somehow it is cheating to use one of the new weight loss medications.

The weight loss saboteurs will still try to sabotage the weight loss of people on the medications as they do for every other method people have employed to achieve a healthy weight. The Fat Monster has not retired. She will still attempt to thwart your efforts to eat moderate portions of healthy food. Her allies in the profit-driven food industry will develop even more tempting, addicting, nutrition-devoid food products and sell them by the cleverest advertising the agencies can devise.

But despite the Puritanical voices, despite the weight loss saboteurs, despite the Fat Monster and the food industry, you can still lose weight and stay slim and healthy. I lost 55 pounds and I have stayed slim more than 55 years.

So can you.

Much Thanks

THROUGHOUT MY STRUGGLES TO WRITE AND PUBLISH my books and to maintain my website I have been fortunate to have good assistance. For this I am extremely grateful.

There would not have been an original *Chic & Slim* book without help and support from my son John. Through the years and subsequent books he has continued that support with advice and editing—and regular batches of "tea reading" to inspire me.

Our *Chic & Slim* Special Correspondent Kat on her frequent visits to France sends back reports and photographs of France, its food, fashion and lifestyle. It was Kat's reports that made me aware of the dramatic cultural changes taking place in France and convinced me that French women (fewer and fewer of them chic and slim) no longer offered us the role models they previously did. Further, Kat's recommendation for Dr. Tim Spector's book *Spoon Fed* introduced me to the gut microbiome and put me on the path to finding a solution to my stress-induced digestive problems.

Susan in Hamilton has continued to send clippings and books with useful information. She ships boxes of wonderful magazines that not only provide ideas for website photos but inspire my remodeling and decorating projects.

Ann Leslie in New York sends information on a multitude of topics for my books and website. Her extensive knowledge of art, music, food and gardening, as well as a variety of esoteric subjects, is invaluable. Additionally, she brings a perspective from another part of the USA much different from my Texas prairie.

Vicki in Friday Harbor shares her eye for good design and sends thoughtful gifts and words of encouragement that aid me in my struggles to write and publish—and to cope with the often hazardous weather that complicates my life.

Rocki in Austin liberally sprinkles French phrases in her cards and emails thus preventing my once quite good command of the French language from fading into oblivion.

Karen in Rosemount who is adept at online research located a company in a nearby town who can repair my old gas cooking stove—if I ever have the budget. She also sends a delightful miscellany of entertaining and amusing information.

From her years of art study Joyce in Griggs understands the importance of proper tools for creativity. She keeps me supplied, not with only encouragement, but with items that stimulate writing and ideas. Joyce also designed the Eiffel Tower logo for the *Chic & Slim* books and website.

And to Susan Who Moves Frequently, though several years ago we somehow lost contact, I hope you are well and enjoying life. The Miranda Esmonde-White book and DVDs have benefited my ageing enormously. I use several of your delightful gifts every day.

I am also grateful to the Baronettes, that faithful group that has continued to read my books and website, including many who have sent useful feedback, gifts, and encouragement through the years.

Resources

Miranda Esmonde-White. The author, anti-ageing educator and ballerina has a variety of books and DVDs, as well as programs you can stream to your television or computer. You can find them on *essentrics.com*. For more than 10 years I have used the information in Miranda Esmonde-White's book *Aging Backwards: Reverse the Aging Process and Look 10 Years Younger in 30 Minutes a Day* and that on her DVD *Classical Stretch by Essentrics Season 10 Strength & Flexibility*. Recently I have began the workouts on *Season 14 Posture Boost & Back Health*.

Twyla Tharp. *Keep It Moving: Lessons for the Rest of Your Life*. The American dancer, choreographer, and author now in her 80s advises that successful ageing demands that we keep moving. Exercise is essential.

Giulia Enders. *Gut: The Inside Story of our Body's Most Underrated Organ*. English translation of a charming little book by the German writer and scientist. The book first published as *Darm mit Charm* (Intestines With Charm) is a bit dated now, but a nice introduction to the gut microbiome.

Chris van Tulleken. *Ultra-Processed People: Why Do We All Eat Stuff That Isn't Food... and Why Can't We Stop?* Dr. van Tulleken is an Oxford-trained British physician who writes and speaks and makes documentaries about how ultra-processed foods and the addiction they create are a cause of the obesity epidemic and have long-term negative effects on our bodies and brains.

Tim Spector. *Food for Life: The New Science of Eating Well*. The book explains the science of the gut microbiome and has a companion cookbook. You can also find many of Dr. Spector's wellness articles on *zoe.com*, the website of the app-delivered nutrition program he co-founded.

Valter Longo. *The Longevity Diet: Slow Aging, Fight Disease, Optimize Weight*. The book lays out an eating plan for a long healthspan. Much information about Dr. Longo's research and his plan for healthy ageing can also be found on *valterlongo.com*.

Anne Barone. *Toujours: Aging Beautifully Like Those Chic French Women* and *Toujours 2: More Aging Beautifully Like Those Chic French Women*. In each new book, I try hard not to repeat information that has appeared in one of my previous books. Much useful information on staying slim and living well for age 65+ not detailed in this book can be found in the two *Toujours*.

For more information
on topics covered in this book
and in the *Chic & Slim* books
visit Anne Barone's supporting website

annebarone.com

www.ingramcontent.com/pod-product-compliance
Lightning Source LLC
Chambersburg PA
CBHW050012040726
47599CB00014B/1344